Programming
Languages
for Micros

For
Nancy & Ben,
Nicholas & Jonathan, and
Frances & Joanne

whose names I have felt free to use here and elsewhere

Programming Languages for Micros

Garry Marshall

Newnes Technical Books

Newnes Technical Books
is an imprint of the Butterworth Group
which has principal offices in
London, Boston, Durban, Singapore, Sydney, Toronto, Wellington

First published 1983

British Library Cataloguing in Publication Data

Marshall, G. J.
   Programming languages for micros.
   1. Microcomputers—Programming
   I. Title
   001.64'24   QA76.73

ISBN 0-408-01185-8

Typeset by Phoenix Photosetting, Chatham
Printed in England by Billing & Sons Ltd., London & Worcester

Preface

I originally learnt several computer languages because both my university, when I was a research student, and my employer for my first job changed their computer fairly often. Since the software changed when the computer did, I had to learn a new programming language quite regularly. Familiarity with Atlas Autocode, Algol and FORTRAN was soon acquired, although, in retrospect, some of my programs could not have done exactly what they were intended to. Since my work involved conventional scientific computing, the subsequent discovery of Lisp was a revelation. At last it became clear to me that computation did not have to be all about numbers and scientific formulae, and that non-numeric computation was possible and there were languages for it.

Having started by learning languages simply to use them, once I had acquired some familiarity with a few of them the fascination of the languages themselves asserted itself. I became aware that they were all providing ways to do the same thing, but that they all embodied different methods of approaching and thinking about it. Of course, if it were possible to program computers in English, no special programming languages would be necessary. But not to have them would be a pity, because the modes of thought embodied in some of them and their abilities to make their users think about problems in ways that they almost certainly would not have done otherwise can make them more stimulating than English. They can guide their users into new areas of thought, whereas English would allow one to drop into established thought patterns. I have found Lisp to be much the most stimulating language in this way.

If computer languages can be exciting in their own right, it is even more exciting to be able to use them on personal computers, and to have the freedom to experiment with them at leisure and without the constraints that mainframe computer usage can impose. Having the opportunity to find out how to express oneself in a particular language and to find out how the language works is stimulating, and possibly quite as interesting as actually applying it to its intended task of describing computations to computers.

This book would not have been possible without the help, direct and indirect, of many people. I should like to thank all the computer managers and programming advisors who have helped to guide me from the paths of programming error, particularly those at the Polytechnic of North London. I am very grateful to Philip Chapman of Newnes Technical Books for giving me the opportunity to write this book and for involving me in the series to which it belongs. The original ideas for the book and the series were his. The book itself grew out of a series of articles published in *Computing Today* and I should like to express my thanks to the editor of that magazine, Henry Budgett, for his prompting and infectious enthusiasm which ensured that the articles were written and, as a further consequence, that this book exists. Finally, I should like to thank my wife, Anne, for her unflagging help and encouragement during the writing of this book.

G.J.M.

Contents

Some example programs
WSFN and micros
COMPUTER-ASSISTED LEARNING (CAL)
  Pilot
    Core Pilot
    Common Pilot
    The success of Pilot as a language for CAL
  Summary
  Self-test questions

Introduction

There is a large and ever increasing number of languages available for microcomputers. A person using a micro for the first time usually encounters a general-purpose language, whether he is writing a program in it or running a program written by someone else. Similarly, the language that is 'built in' to a micro, or that is initially provided with one, tends to be general purpose. A general-purpose language is one in which any kind of computation can be described to a computer so that it can perform that computation.

Now, an almost universal trend, in which micro users are in no way different from mainframe computer users, is that once a user becomes interested and involved in writing programs for some particular special purpose he becomes dissatisfied with the general-purpose language and looks for a language that is more specialised and therefore more suited to his needs. People failing to find a suitable specialist language have been known to devise one for themselves! The trend towards the use of special-purpose languages is in no way surprising since it is entirely equivalent to the situation of the workman who acquires particular tools for special jobs and who can, as a consequence, perform those tasks more quickly and more effectively by using the tools best suited to them.

So languages exist for most of the specialist activities in which micros are used. By examining these languages and the areas in which they find application it is possible to find out how micros are used and what they are used for. Thus this book can, almost incidentally, provide the answers to questions such as 'What are micros used for?' and 'What can I do with my micro?' It will emerge that there are languages for establishing and interrogating databases, for writing computer-assisted learning packages, and for controlling robots. Also, that there are languages intended particularly for business applications, for Artificial Intelligence, and even for writing programs that help the user to write his own programs.

It seems to me particularly important to satisfy the new, or potential, user of a micro when he asks what the micro can be used for. Without a satisfactory answer he may never develop an interest in micros at all, and may consequently never appreciate the way in which he could use one to advantage. Besides this, people approaching a micro for the first time can start with strong misconceptions of what it can do and how it does it. Some seem to believe that there is an element of magic involved. Attempting to explain the first steps in programming in BASIC to such a person can present him with something he is quite unable to relate to his mistaken preconceived ideas and leave him completely disillusioned.

If I have managed to give the impression that this book is about *using* a micro, then I have succeeded in expressing my aim. The book is not concerned with the hardware, the electronics and technology, of micros, but only with how to use them. A micro can be used to good effect to run an existing program such as one designed to aid in making business decisions. This book is not so much concerned with using a micro in this way as with using it creatively. The way to use it creatively is to program it to do what you want it to do. This could be to use it to test your own ideas, to try out different ways of doing things, to educate yourself or your family, or even (dare one say it) to make some money.

To the user wondering what to use a micro for, then, this book should give some ideas. The user who knows what he wants to use a micro for may find this book of help in giving some ideas as to how to go about it and, besides this, it may also suggest the direction in which the next step can be taken by indicating an appropriate specialist software tool and how it is used.

1
Introduction to computer languages

What is a programming language?

A natural language such as English or French is used by people to communicate with each other. The purpose of any programming language is, similarly, to provide a means of communication. It enables solution methods or procedures for achieving some specific objective to be described to a computer in a *precise* way. The difficulties in communicating with a computer using a natural language stem largely from its inherent ambiguity and lack of precision. Of course, natural languages permit the expression of a tremendous variety of shades of meaning, and computer languages cannot compete with them on this score.

The ambiguity of natural language is illustrated by sentences such as:

Smoking cigarettes can be dangerous.
Hatching the egg caused grave problems.
The peasants are revolting.
The dense population of Manchester was growing restless.

The first example could mean that smoking cigarettes is dangerous (if you must do it) or that smoking cigarettes are dangerous (if you leave them lying around). The last example was probably not meant to be rude to Mancunians.

A computer cannot guarantee to interpret and respond to an ambiguous communication in the way that is intended by the sender of the communication. It may be able to take one of its meanings, but that may not be the one intended. People resolve the ambiguity of a communication expressed in natural language by relating the message to its context. Computers can be programmed to do this, but the representation of the information in the message and the inclusion of all the knowledge that is likely to be required to provide a context for the ambiguous message are complex problems from the Artificial Intelligence area. The techniques are currently the subject of research investigations. They may come into common use in the future, but they are not presently at a stage where they can be commonly employed.

Another aspect of the problem of ambiguity in understanding natural languages stems from the richness of the grammatical rules for constructing correct sentences. This richness leads to sentences like the following pair:

Time flies like an arrow.
Fruit flies like a banana.

Both sentences are meaningful. Their deceptive similarity conceals different grammatical constructions. Determining the structure of a sentence (its syntax) is a necessary preliminary to finding its meaning, but being sure of this structure can be difficult. In fact, the essential reason for the ambiguity of the sentence

Flying planes can be dangerous.

is that it conforms to two different grammatical constructions, both of which are perfectly valid.

Besides the question of structure, there is also the question of the meaning of a sentence (the semantics). In a natural language it is possible to invent properly structured sentences that are entirely meaningless, such as Chomsky's

Colourless green ideas dream furiously.

What could a computer do with a structurally correct command (that is, one with no syntax errors) that means absolutely nothing?

Syntax and semantics are not the only concerns when dealing with languages. With a spoken natural language, for example, *phonology* (the system of sounds in the language) is also a concern. In a spoken language there is a logic to the way in which sounds can be combined, so that certain combinations of sounds make valid words and sentences, and others do not. Also, by speaking the sentence

The man made a bow.

it could be determined if he had bent at the waist or had made something to fire his arrows with. To this extent, the meaning of the sentence could be determined although, unfortunately, the latter case would still not be distinguished from the situation where the man had just tied his shoe laces. With a programming language, the *pragmatics* are a third matter of concern. The pragmatic aspects of a programming language relate to how easily it can be implemented for a particular computer and to how well it supports good methods of writing programs.

Programming languages are designed as artificial languages with comparatively simple grammatical rules so that all the problems which have been outlined above can be avoided. Thus, when com-

4

municating with a computer in a programming language, a programmer can be sure of how the computer will respond when it executes the instructions it is given. There will be no ambiguity. The structure and meaning of each instruction will be unique. There will be no 'nonsense' instructions. Every legally constructed instruction will be interpreted precisely in the way that it should be, and the result should be exactly what the programmer intended. Given a particular, legal, program there can be no doubt about how the computer will respond to it: the one essential is that the programmer should describe the task in hand precisely.

High-level languages and microcomputers

High-level languages are programming languages that are intended for people to use, whereas low-level languages are oriented to the computer. The lowest language level of all is the so-called machine code of a computer, which is the language that it responds to directly. It gives direct access to all the resources of a computer. While programs written in machine code are best suited to the computer, they are totally unsuited to people: they consist of strings of binary digits and as such are both unstructured and unreadable. High-level languages are designed to permit a logical structure to be given to programs and to make them readable.

Now machine codes have existed since the first electronic computers were invented. The first high-level language came into general use in 1957. The first micros that sold in large numbers appeared in Britain in 1977, although they were in evidence rather earlier than this in America. So by the time that the first micros appeared a number of high-level languages had been in use for some years. The designers of microcomputers naturally took advantage of this by borrowing languages from the conventional computer world.

The choice of language for all the first generation micros that sold in large numbers, including the PET, Apple and TRS80, was BASIC. The reasons for adopting BASIC are not hard to find. The main one is that it is easy to learn and to use. Thus, having acquired a micro, the owner can learn its programming language and then start to program it in a fairly short time. By the same token, a body of programs for micros could quickly be built up. In fact, companies selling programs written by, and for, micro users, and paying a royalty to the program writer, quickly sprang into existence. They met a demand for programs from micro users, and in that way helped to promote the popularity of microcomputers. Thirdly, BASIC, in its simplicity, provided an ideal medium for exchanging programs either directly or through the popular computing magazines. BASIC was devised in an academic institution as a computer language that would be easy to learn and to teach, but it came ready-made as a godsend to the microcomputer world.

BASIC continues as the language chosen for microcomputers aimed at a broad range of users, being the language of, for example, the Sinclair ZX81, the Acorn Atom and the BBC Microcomputer.

While BASIC is the most widely used general-purpose language on micros, it does have shortcomings that can become apparent in certain circumstances. In particular, BASIC makes it difficult to give a coherent structure to large programs. Consequently, the tasks of developing, amending and adapting long programs written in BASIC can be more arduous than is really necessary. For these reasons, and others, Pascal has been used increasingly as a general-purpose language for micros, and it is at present the only language to rival BASIC. Within some specialised communities of users it is more widely used than BASIC. Pascal insists that programs be developed in a systematic way, and permits them to be given a clear and simple structure. Thus, the Pascal programmer finds that the language imposes certain disciplines, but the result is that large programs whose meaning is clear and which possess a logical structure can be written. As a consequence, Pascal is rather harder to learn than BASIC, not least because there is rather more to learn before writing the first program. However, the benefits that can be obtained can make the extra effort worthwhile. It is an interesting fact that Pascal, like BASIC, was devised in an academic institution.

Many other languages have been taken from the conventional computer world by users of microcomputers. In some instances their use is attractive because a large body of useful programs has already been written in that language. Another reason has been that enthusiasts want to use a language that is particularly suited to their specialist activity.

To demonstrate that the microcomputer world is not completely parasitic in the matter of programming languages it must be mentioned that languages have been developed for micros and, ironically, that users of larger computers have shown a good deal of interest in them! To cite one example, COMAL has been devised as a language intermediate between BASIC and Pascal which would be as easy to learn as the former while giving the benefits of the latter.

Translators

The electronic 'heart' of a microcomputer is a microprocessor. In a sense, the rest of the microcomputer is there to make the capabilities

6

of the microprocessor readily available to the user. A microprocessor can perform a limited range of rather simple operations: typical operations are moving data from one place to another, and adding two numbers together. The 6502 microprocessor, found in the PET and Apple (to name but two), has a repertoire of some 50 operations. The Z80 microprocessor used in, for example, the Sharp MZ80K, has a larger repertoire; it includes operations similar to, although rarely exactly the same as, those of the 6502.

Now the machine code of a microprocessor consists of the set of instructions which command the microprocessor to perform each of the operations in its repertoire. The microprocessor can respond directly only to these intructions, and only to them when they are expressed, in coded form, as strings of binary digits. One advantage of programming in a high-level language should be apparent at this point; whereas programs written in machine code will only run on certain machines, programs written in a high-level language should run on any machine.

Since a microprocessor cannot understand BASIC, Pascal or anything other than its own machine code, the question arises as to how a microcomputer runs programs written in a high-level language. The answer is that it must possess the capability not only to accept programs written in a high-level language but also to translate them to machine code before they are run. The translator is referred to as either an 'interpreter' or a 'compiler' depending on how it carries out the translation.

An interpreter takes one line of a high-level language program, translates it, and the resulting machine code instructions are executed before the interpreter proceeds to the next line which is treated in the same way. A compiler translates a complete program written in a high-level language to a complete machine code program before it is run. The two kinds of translator show to advantage in different circumstances. When trying to correct a faulty program, an interpreter deals satisfactorily with each correct line in the program but halts the execution of the program as soon as it comes to a faulty line, thus locating an error in the program, which can then be corrected. A compiler is usually not so helpful in correcting faults, but it runs a correct program much more quickly than an interpreter. In this way, an interpreter is more useful while a program is being developed, and a compiler saves time when running fully developed programs.

The translator itself, be it an interpreter or a compiler, is essentially a computer program which accepts a program written in a high-level language as its input and which produces a machine code program describing the same computation as its output. Examining the translators available for some of the popular micros shows that they can take various forms. The BASIC interpreter for the PET is stored in permanent form in chips installed in the machine, and it automatically becomes available when the machine is switched on. To introduce some jargon, the translator in this case is stored in read-only memory (ROM); that is, in a memory that can be consulted but cannot be changed in any way. With the Sharp MZ80K the BASIC translator is supplied on cassette. It is loaded into the machine by using the cassette unit to copy the translator from the cassette tape to the machine's memory. In this case it is copied into random access memory (RAM); that is, memory whose contents can be consulted and also changed. To help distinguish between RAM and ROM, it can be noted that if a PET is turned off and then on again, its BASIC is still available because it is in permanent memory, whereas the Sharp's BASIC would have vanished and would have to be loaded again. In case this partial information about the PET and Sharp appears biased towards the PET, it should be noted that Pascal can be loaded into the Sharp from a cassette just as easily as BASIC can.

So translators can be stored in ROM or on a permanent magnetic medium, in which case they must be transferred to RAM before they are used. Translators, including some for Pascal (with one for the PET), are also stored on floppy disk. Again, they are loaded into memory as required. One characteristic of disk usage is that information can be transferred very rapidly between disk unit and computer. Taking advantage of this, the whole translation system need not be transferred to the computer's memory, but only the part that is currently required. When another part is needed, e.g. to deal with an error situation, it can be transferred from the disk to perform its function. In this way translation systems that take up more storage than the computer has available at any one time can be used.

Hopefully, it is clear that translation is fundamental to the use of a high-level language. A language is *implemented* on a particular machine by writing a translator that can translate any program written in that language to a program describing the same computation in the machine code of that machine. Since translators are themselves programs, and must be stored in the computer before they can be used, they occupy a certain amount of the computer's memory. Given two translators that can translate equally well, one of them could be considered better if it occupied less store, that is, if it were more compact. One reason that some languages used on mainframe computers have not been implemented at all for micros is that their translators require too much storage. Other languages have not been fully implemented for the same reason. That is to say, in order to keep the memory requirement of the translator within bounds, certain features of the language have been omitted so that the translator can only deal with a sub-set of the complete language.

In discussing the ideas involved in the implementation of a language, it is implicitly assumed that the language itself is fixed. In other words, whatever BASIC is, for example, it is the same for everybody. Now this is actually not the case as almost anyone who has tried to run a BASIC program on just about any two different micros can confirm. This brings us to the problem of *standardisation*. Attempts to standardise programming languages were made long before the advent of micros. In fact, FORTRAN became the first high-level language to acquire a standard form from a national standards authority. If programs written in a high-level language are to be portable, in the sense that a program that runs on one machine with the appropriate translator will run on any other similarly equipped machine, then standardisation is obviously necessary.

The situation concerning the standardisation of BASIC is particularly vexed. Attempts to standardise it preceded its use on micros, but the adoption of BASIC by micros has made the situation much worse. The designers of micros have been, to say the least, cavalier in their attitudes to any standard. Clearly, the priorities of the designers have been to have an implementation for their own machines, but the frustrations that can be caused by a lack of standardisation are met by any micro user who finds a program to do exactly what he wants published in a magazine only to realise subsequently that it is written in the dialect of BASIC used by a machine other than his own. This situation is so prevalent that at least one book has been written simply showing how to convert programs from one dialect of BASIC to another.

There may be good reasons for a lack of standardisation in a rapidly evolving field. As an example, micros with highly individual graphics facilities may well require extra commands to make those facilities readily accessible. However, there is a real advantage in having a standardised core to a language, so that all BASICs contain the same core, but have extra features added on as necessary.

Features and applications

One language will be used in a particular application in preference to others because it is better suited to that application. Probably it is better suited because it possesses features that are particularly relevant or which make it easier to describe the required computations. At any rate, there is an interplay between the features that a language possesses and the applications to which it is applied.

A general-purpose language should permit programs to be written to describe any computation whatever, so the question arises as to what features a language should possess in order to allow this. It should certainly permit data to be stored, and not only numbers but also characters or text. It should also allow that data to be manipulated, so that numerical operations can be performed on numbers, and characters can be manipulated as well. Most languages have constructs that facilitate the description of computations: those usually provided include selection, repetition and grouping. Additionally, it is usual to be able to construct sub-programs that can be invoked easily by a main program, perhaps to save writing out a much needed procedure every time it is required, or to construct a tool needed by a particular program that is not itself provided by the language.

This compilation of features that should be possessed by a general-purpose language is of necessity rather vague: the details for specific languages will in any case be presented in subsequent chapters. The theory of computability shows that it is possible to compute anything that is computable with surprisingly little machinery, which in turn requires only a small number of commands. (The Turing machine, defined by the English mathematician A. M.Turing in 1936, shows exactly what is required.) Without going into the theory of computability at all, it is sufficient to observe that all high-level languages possess more than the minimum that is necessary in order to describe any computation. So the relevant question, in this context, is not whether a high-level language can be used to describe a computation but whether the language is particularly convenient for describing it.

As to whether one language is better than another, I hope we can agree that this is a meaningless question. While one language may be better than another in a particular application it is doubtful that this superiority can be maintained across a wide range of applications. The information on languages for micros presented in subsequent chapters may help the reader to decide whether a particular language is worth learning, whether it will be useful in a specific application or simply that languages other than a familiar one may be worth investigation.

What is different about microcomputing?

That this book is about high-level languages for microcomputers carries the implication that computing with a micro is in some way different from other ways of computing. However, a micro operates in essentially the same way as any other computer; its major distinguishing feature is its smallness, which results from the technology employed in fabricating its electronic components, mainly the microprocessor and memories. To express this crudely, a micro works in the same way as other computers, but is made differently. We have already seen that programs for micros are often written in the languages used by other computers. To this degree, computing with a micro is in the mainstream of computing.

Differences can be observed when the ways in which micros are applied are considered. The fact that a micro is small makes it portable, so that it can be used in remote or confined places where a large computer could not, even from a terminal. On remote archaeological sites micros are used to record the finds, and in cramped circumstances, in a mine for example, they are used to monitor environmental conditions and to control experiments. The cheapness of a micro makes it possible for the enthusiast to have one to use in any way that he may like. Equally, it makes it possible to use one in a small business for purposes such as stock control or payroll calculations. Micros are also sufficiently cheap to be used in laboratories as special-purpose devices for calibration, and for monitoring or controlling experiments.

Because micros are so cheap, the user can have one to himself, in contrast to the situation with a large machine which is generally so expensive that it must be shared. Having exclusive use of the machine the user can delve into its innermost workings, exploring how it works and how the programs that control it operate. Such things are definitely frowned on when using large machines, not least because they can affect the machines' other users. In a similar way, there is less inhibition about attaching external devices to micros. While printers and magnetic storage devices are likely to be attached to any computer, one is much more likely to find robot arms or small robot devices attached to a micro.

In the home, the cheap and portable micro is going to become part of an information system giving access not only to Teletext and Prestel, and enhancing their facilities, but also to information banks held by other computers. The potential of the micro as an educational aid has not been fully tapped yet. Both in the home and in educational institutions it becomes a very real learning and teaching aid, given suitable programs to run on it.

Some of the applications for micros that have been mentioned are new, and some are not. What *is* new is the range of people who can afford to use a computer to do work for them, help them or merely entertain them. Additionally, micros can now be used profitably for tasks that previously could not have possibly been achieved economically with a computer. Since micros make possible such diverse activities as teaching children to master complex ideas in a pleasurable way, and running small robot-controlled manufacturing facilities in the garden shed, it is not only computing that they have changed.

Summary and further reading

This chapter has discussed in a general way high-level languages, their characteristics and their areas of application. The need for translation has been stressed, because finally a computer can only execute programs written in its own machine code so that programs written in any other language must be translated to this form. The high-level languages that are used with microcomputers have been indicated together with typical applications in which they are used. After showing that computing with a micro is, in essence, no different from any other form of computing, an attempt has been made to show how micros are applied differently. The different applications often become possible, or viable, as a result of the smallness and the cheapness of the micro.

The following books are suggested for further reading on some of the topics touched on in this chapter.

Programming languages: history and fundamentals, by Jean Sammet (Prentice-Hall, 1969)
This book gives an exhaustive listing of all the languages implemented up to 1969, a date well before the advent of micros. It illustrates very well the variety of computer languages and the diversity of their characteristics.

Programming language standardisation, edited by I. D. Hill and B. L. Meek (Ellis Horwood, 1980)
The problems, politics and even the successes of standardisation are described in this book.

Principles of programming languages, by R. D. Tennent (Prentice-Hall, 1981)
The fundamental concepts and general principles of programming languages are explained in this text. A certain amount of background and experience is necessary in order to read it, but it provides many insights.

I hesitate to give a reference to the theory of computation, since it is a highly mathematical subject not lending itself to easy reading. However, almost any book with the words 'theory of computation' or 'computability' in its title will be found to cover the subject.

2
The major microcomputer languages

The most commonly used high-level languages on micros are BASIC and Pascal. BASIC is the original microcomputer language, having the great asset of being easy to learn. It has now acquired the status of being *the* microcomputer language for beginners and hobbyists because of its ready availability for all machines and also because, as a consequence of its use for several years, there are large numbers of programs in BASIC and many books about it. However, BASIC does have shortcomings, most of which become apparent when developing large programs. Pascal has become the preferred language for use where BASIC is less than satisfactory, and it is also available for practically every micro. Actually, Pascal is being adopted for program development in other areas too, including mainframe usage and microprocessor systems development. Both BASIC and Pascal were devised in academic institutions where their originators identified particular requirements of general computer users, which also happen to be the needs of micro users, and designed the languages accordingly.

The aims of this chapter are to indicate, for both BASIC and Pascal, the way in which computations can be described, what typical programs are like, and to describe the applications in which they generally appear.

BASIC

BASIC was devised by J. G. Kemeny and T. E. Kertz of Dartmouth College in the USA. It was designed as an interactive language that would be easy to learn and to teach as a result of an English-like appearance. It first became available in 1965. There are many varied versions of BASIC available now, and they can show considerable differences from each other. However, the dialect known as Microsoft BASIC has almost come to be accepted as the standard for microcomputers, and by staying fairly close to this version it is possible to give a description of BASIC that is similar to that available on most micros.

Fundamentally, computers store and process information. Initially, we shall examine the simple ways to do these things in BASIC. A number can be stored by giving a command such as

LET   A=3

This can be read as 'store the number 3 in a location in the memory which is to be called A'. The command is obeyed as soon as it is given: its effect is illustrated in *Fig. 2.1a*. On most micros it is permissible, and usual, to abbreviate the command to

A=3

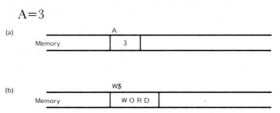

Fig. 2.1. The effects of assignments (a) A=3 (b) W$="WORD"

Some machines, including the Sinclair ZX81, insist that the LET be present, but in the remainder of this section it will be omitted. Note that the command is an assignment and that it is *not* an equation. BASIC also permits letters, characters and words to be stored: this can be done by

W$="WORD"

which can be read as 'store the string of characters W, O, R and D in a part of the memory and call it W$'. The effect of this is illustrated in *Fig. 2.1b*.

BASIC deals with only numbers and strings of letters. The $ symbol must be added to the name allocated to the region where a string of characters is stored so that BASIC can distinguish the contents from a number. More complicated kinds of data must be handled by the programmer in terms of these two types.

When these two commands given above are issued, there is no external sign that anything has happened: to demonstrate that it has, we need to examine the memory locations where items are stored. For this purpose BASIC provides the PRINT command, and

PRINT A

for example, can be read as 'print the contents of the location called A'. In this case it gives the result

3

The command

PRINT W$

produces the output

WORD

Numbers can be processed using the normal arithmetic operations. The symbols for the operations are summarised in Table 2.1. Now two numbers can be stored and their sum printed out by giving, successively, the following three commands:

A=2.5
B=6.0
PRINT A+B

Table 2.1. Operators: their symbols and meanings

	With numbers
+	addition
−	subtraction
*	multiplication
/	division
↑	exponentiation (raising to the power)
	With words
+	concatenation (adding second word to first)

Each command is obeyed as soon as it is given, and the third command generates the result

8.5

At this stage we can write our first program. The program to store two numbers and print their sum is obtained by preceding each of the commands given above by a line number. The order of the numbers gives the order in which the commands are to be carried out when the program is run. Thus, the program could be

1   A=2.5
2   B=6.0
3   PRINT A+B
4   END

The end of the program listing is usually indicated by an END command, although on some machines it is not necessary to have it. When the instructions (consisting of a line number and a command) are entered, they are stored: they are *not* obeyed at this time. When the lines are entered, the command

LIST

will cause the stored program to be listed, demonstrating that it has in fact been stored. To execute the program it is necessary to give the command

RUN

The instructions in the program will then be executed in the order given by their line numbers. However, after this the program is still stored, so that it can be listed and run again. It is more usual to see the program lines numbered as follows:

```
10   A=2.5
20   B=6.0
30   PRINT A+B
40   END
```

The line numbers indicate the same order for the execution of the commands but are more generously spaced. This permits further lines to be inserted between program lines should it be necessary to amplify the program, whereas in the previous program it would be necessary to re-enter lines with new line numbers.

Arithmetic expressions such as

A+2 * B

can be constructed using the arithmetic operators, and brackets can be used as required, for example:

(A+B)/(A+B)

If brackets are not used to indicate the meaning of an expression such as

A * B ↑ 3+6

then the following rules apply:

1. Raising to a power is done first.
2. Multiplication and division are done next.
3. Addition and subtraction are done last.
4. When multiplications and divisions appear together they are done in turn from left to right.
5. When additions and subtractions appear together they are done in turn from left to right.

These rules are really only the normal ones which apply to arithmetic expressions. Generally, in a complicated expression it is better to use brackets if there is any doubt that the expression may not be evaluated in the intended way.

The general form of a numerical assignment is

variable=arithmetic expression

The left-hand side of the assignment must be simply a variable name, while the right-hand side can be any properly formed arithmetic expression. In this way any arithmetic calculations can be performed with stored numbers and the numbers that are explicitly included in the arithmetic expressions. A simple program to illustrate this which stores three numbers, finds their average, their product and the ratio of the difference of the first two numbers to the last two before printing out the results is given below.

```
10   A =5.5
20   B =6.7
30   C =3.3
40   M=(A+B+C)/3
50   P =A * B * C
60   D =(A−B)/(B−C)
70   PRINT M, P, D
80   END
```

At this point we can write BASIC programs to do problems comparable to those that can be tackled using a four-function calculator, but we are only at the beginning and we shall progress a good deal further.

The '+' operator can be used with words, as well as numbers, and in this context it denotes concatenation. To illustrate, after the pair of assignments

R$="REACT"
I$ ="IONS"

the command

PRINT R$+I$

gives

REACTIONS

Other ways of manipulating words will be described later.

Improvements

The last program that was presented, although it does what was intended, can be improved considerably. It prints its results simply as three numbers; this may be satisfactory for the person who wrote the program and who knows what it does, but it is not helpful to anyone else. BASIC permits this situation to be improved by allowing PRINT to be used in a way in which it can print out a pre-set message. Thus, we could add to the program the line

65 PRINT "THE AVERAGE, PRODUCT AND DIFFER
ENCE RATIO ARE"

to identify the results. Used in this way, PRINT causes exactly what is between the associated inverted commas to be printed.

Also, the program only deals with the numbers stored by the assignments in its first three lines. The program would be more useful if it dealt with any three numbers, but to do this the first three lines in the program must be changed every time. However, BASIC provides a feature with which any number can be entered when the program is run: this is INPUT. It works in the following way: the program line

10 INPUT A

will, when it is executed, cause a prompting sign (usually a question mark) to be printed, and then make the program wait until a number is entered. When a number is entered it is stored in A. If the question mark is not found to be a good enough prompt, the programmer can always print his own prompting message.

In this way the following improved program can be obtained

```
 5   PRINT "ENTER THE FIRST NUMBER"
10   INPUT A
15   PRINT "ENTER THE SECOND NUMBER"
20   INPUT B
25   PRINT "ENTER THE THIRD NUMBER"
30   INPUT C
40   M=(A+B+C)/3
50   P =A * B * C
60   D =(A−B)/(B−C)
65   PRINT "THE AVERAGE, PRODUCT AND DIFFER
     ENCE RATIO ARE"
70   PRINT M, P, D
80   END
```

A typical dialogue produced by running this program is

ENTER THE FIRST NUMBER
?   5.0

ENTER THE SECOND NUMBER
? 3.0
ENTER THE THIRD NUMBER
? 2.0
THE AVERAGE, PRODUCT AND DIFFERENCE RATIO ARE
3.3333333   30.0   2.0

Programming structures

BASIC provides very few structures for the convenience of the programmer in building programs. This is part of the reason that
BASIC is so easy to learn—other languages tend to provide larger
repertoires. It is also a large factor in determining the characteristic
flavour of BASIC programs; they all have to be built using the same
small number of building blocks.

Two of the structures provided by BASIC are for decision-making
and for repetition. The structure for decision-making is the conditional instruction, which has the form

IF condition THEN command

The condition part typically consists of a test involving the comparison of two values, while the command part can be any BASIC
command except, usually, another conditional one. When executed,
the condition part is tested, and if the test shows the condition to be
true then the command in the command part is executed, otherwise
it is not. Typical examples of conditional instructions are

IF A$="SMITH" THEN PRINT "WHICH SMITH IS
THIS?"

which causes the enquiry about which Smith to be printed only if the
word stored in A$ is SMITH, and

IF X>17 THEN Y=X+32

which causes the assignment to Y to be made only if the number
stored in X exceeds 17. In this way, the conditional instruction provides a means by which the computer can automatically decide
whether or not to execute a command at a particular point in a program by making a specified test.

The repeated execution of a task is facilitated by the structure
which includes the two BASIC words FOR and NEXT. All the
instructions placed between these two words are executed repeatedly as many times as directed by the information attached to FOR.
A notice can be printed 15 times by

```
10   FOR I=1 TO 15
20   PRINT "NO SMOKING"
30   NEXT I
```

This causes NO SMOKING to be printed first when I=1, next when I=2, and so on until it is finally done with I=15.

A program fragment to accept eight numbers and print them out is

```
10   FOR K=1 TO 8
20   INPUT A
30   PRINT "ENTRY", K, "IS", A
40   NEXT K
```

Although BASIC makes the repeated execution of instructions easy, it provides the facility in such a way that it is necessary to pre-scribe the exact number of repetitions. In many tasks this is neither possible nor desirable, as for example in any data entry and processing task where the amount of data to be processed is unpredictable and may vary from one use of the program to the next. Consider the task of writing a program to accept a password and to allow further use of the program only when the correct password is given as illustrated in *Fig. 2.2.* Only one attempt to give the password should be required, but allowance must be made for wrongly keyed entries and other possible errors. The use of the standard repetition facility is not entirely appropriate here, but a suitable program can be written using GOTO. The effect of the command

GOTO 90

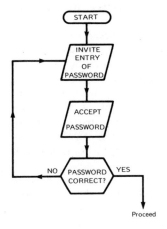

Fig. 2.2.   Password acceptor

20

is to cause the computer to go to line 90 and to execute that line next. The 'acceptor' program can now be written as

```
10  PRINT "ENTER PASSWORD"
20  INPUT A$
30  IF A$<>"TRUE PASSWORD" THEN GOTO 10
40  PRINT "WELCOME. THE PROGRAM IS READY TO
    USE"
```

.
.
.

The pair of symbols $<>$ in line 30 mean 'not equal to'. Lines 10 to 30 will be repeated until the correct password is given, and the number of times they are repeated can be anything from one upwards.

The GOTO instruction is a centre of controversy when it comes to considering methods of writing programs. Its careless use can lead to unnecessary jumping about during the execution of a program; it will also make programs difficult to read and to understand. However, in BASIC the use of GOTO is often essential. In a language such as Pascal, as we shall see, the structures provided by the language are such that it is not necessary to use GOTO at all.

The 'shapes' provided for program building by the BASIC constructs for conditional execution and for repetition are illustrated in *Figs. 2.3a* and *b*.

The other major programming structure provided by BASIC is the subroutine which it offers as its sub-program facility. A subroutine is a sub-program which itself describes a computation: if this computation is required several times in the course of a program then the subroutine can be called each time rather than having to write out all the instructions describing the computation every time. The lines of a subroutine are numbered in the same way as are those of a program. The BASIC words for handling a subroutine are GOSUB and RETURN. A subroutine is called in a main program by GOSUB followed by the line number of the first line in the subroutine,

GOSUB 2000

for example. This command acts like GOTO 2000, but in addition it causes the line number of the next line in the main program to be stored. The command

RETURN

is placed at the end of a subroutine: because the place in the main program to which the return should occur has been recorded, the

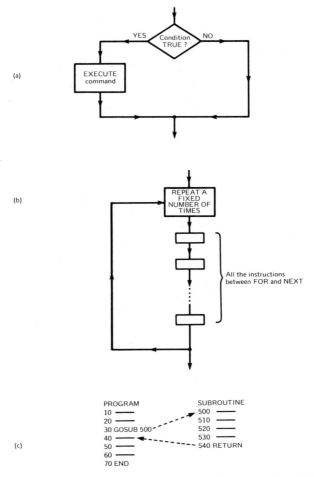

Fig. 2.3. 'Shapes' for program construction (a) IF condition THEN command (b) Repetition with FOR–NEXT (c) SUBROUTINE

automatic return to the correct place can occur. The subroutine 'shape', or the way in which a program and subroutine are linked, is illustrated in *Fig. 2.3c*.

An example of a program which calls a subroutine to add a decorative box to its printed results in several places is given below.

```
10   A$="NANCY"
20   B$="BEN"
30   GOSUB 500
```

```
40   PRINT A$
50   GOSUB 500
60   PRINT B$
70   GOSUB 500
80   STOP
500  PRINT "******"
510  PRINT "*    *"
520  PRINT "******"
530  RETURN
540  END
```

In this program STOP denotes where the computation should halt whereas END shows the physical end of the program listing. When run, the program gives its results in the following form:

```
******
*    *
******
NANCY
******
*    *
******
BEN
******
*    *
******
```

In any language, subprograms can be used to give structure to a large program. By dividing a large task into sub-tasks in a logical way, a coherent structure can be imposed on the task and consequently on the program describing how to accomplish it. Programs with good structure are easier to read, understand and amend than those lacking it.

Functions

BASIC possesses a range of functions: it includes numerical functions broadly comparable to those possessed by a scientific calculator and functions for handling characters. Since the latter are probably less familiar, they are described first.

The function LEN gives the number of letters in a word or, what is the same, the number of characters in a character string. Thus, after the assignment

N$="NANCY"

the command

PRINT LEN (N$)

which can be read as 'print the number of letters in the word stored in N$', gives the result

5

We have already seen how to add characters together and, to complement this, BASIC provides the functions LEFT$, RIGHT$ and MID$ for taking them apart. The names of the functions are indicative of their purposes, which are summarised in Table 2.2.

Table 2.2. BASIC string handling functions

Form of function	Given by function
LEFT$ (N$,3)	The left-hand three characters of the character string stored in N$
RIGHT$ (C$,2)	The right-hand two characters of the character string stored in C$
MID$ (E$,4,5)	The string of characters in the middle of E$ which starts with the fourth character and is five characters long

To illustrate the use of these commands, after the assignment

N$="NETHERLANDS"

the results produced by a sequence of commands are given below:

PRINT LEFT$ (N$,6)

NETHER

PRINT RIGHT$ (N$,5)

LANDS

PRINT MID$ (N$, 2,5)

ETHER

PRINT MID$ (N$,3,3)

THE

PRINT MID$ (N$,4,1)+MID$ (N$,8,3)

HAND

The following program will generate a triangular pattern of stars.

```
10  S$="******"
20  N=LEN (S$)
```

```
30    FOR I=1 TO N
40    PRINT LEFT$ (S$,I)
50    NEXT I
60    END
```

The pattern is

```
*
**
***
****
*****
******
```

The triangle can be inverted by changing line 30 to

30 FOR I=N TO 1 STEP −1

which will cause the repetitions to start with I=N (6 in this case) and then change I by −1 to 5 for the second repetition and so on until the last repetition is done with I=1. The step is taken as 1 in FOR-NEXT repetitions unless it is indicated that it is something else.

Table 2.3. Numerical functions normally provided by BASIC

Form of function	Given by function
ABS(X)	Absolute value of X eg ABS(−2) is 2
INT(X)	Integer part of X eg INT(1.5) is 1
COS(X)	Cosine of X, with X taken in radians
EXP(X)	e^x
LOG(X)	The natural logarithm of X
RND	A random number between 0 and 1
SIN(X)	Sine of X, with X taken in radians
SQR(X)	The square root of X eg SQR(4) is 2
FRE	The amount of unused memory available to the user

The use of the functions listed in Table 2.3 is illustrated by the following program for generating a table of sine and cosine values. Note that line 50 in the program is included to convert X to radians before it is used by the sine and cosine functions

```
10    PI=3.14159265
20    C=PI/180
30    PRINT "X(DEGREES)", "SIN(X)", "COS(X)"
```

```
40   FOR I=0 TO 90
50   X=I*C
60   PRINT I, SIN(X), COS(X)
70   NEXT I
80   END
```

Structuring data

When handling data, particularly in large amounts, it is useful to be able to structure it so that it can be handled in a logical and sensible way. The only facility provided by BASIC for structuring data is the *array*. An array is essentially a set of variables which can be accessed using an index. The BASIC command

DIM A(12)

creates 12 variables named A(1) to A(12): it also reserves space in memory for them. These variables can be treated in the same way as any others; for example, both

A(7)=5

and

X=A(6)+A(12)

are perfectly valid assignments.

The array is ideally suited for use with the repetition facility. If a 12-element array is to be used for holding the monthly sales figures of a business concern, then the figures can be entered as follows

```
10   DIM M(12)
20   FOR I=1 TO 12
30   PRINT "ENTER SALES FIGURE FOR MONTH", I
40   INPUT M(I)
50   NEXT I
```

A histogram to represent the figures could be drawn by adding

```
60   S$="**********"
70   FOR I=1 TO 12
80   PRINT LEFT$(S$,M(I))
90   NEXT I
```

The month in which the most sales were made could be identified by adding

```
100   X=M(1)
110   K=1
```

```
120   FOR J=2 TO 12
130   IF M(J)<X THEN GOTO 160
140   X=M(J)
150   K=J
160   NEXT J
170   PRINT "THE HIGHEST SALES WERE IN MONTH",
      K
```

It is also possible to have arrays of character variables. The following program shows how a group of words can be stored in an array and then sorted into the order in which they would appear in a dictionary. After sorting, the first element of the array will have been assigned the word to be found nearest the beginning of the dictionary, and so on.

```
10    DIM W$ (10)
20    FOR K=1 TO 10
30    PRINT "ENTER WORD"
40    INPUT W$(K)
50    NEXT K
60    FOR I=1 TO 9
70    FOR J=(I+1) TO 10
80    IF W$(I)<W$(J) THEN GOTO 120
90    T$=W$(I)
100   W$(I)=W$(J)
110   W$(J)=T$
120   NEXT J
130   NEXT I
140   END
```

PEEK and POKE

Microcomputer BASICs provide the PEEK and POKE commands with which the contents of the memory can be examined and changed. On most popular micros the memory is partitioned into eight-bit locations. Consequently the contents of a location can be any binary number from 00000000 to 11111111, which corresponds in decimal to the range of numbers from 0 to 255. (Note that $255=2^8-1$) Microprocessors such as the 6502 and Z80, used in popular microcomputers, not only have eight-bit data lines but also 16-bit address lines. They can therefore address $2^{16}=64K=65,536$ memory locations in the memory of a micro. The operating system and BASIC will occupy part of this memory, so that the whole 64K is not available to the user for storing programs and data.

A number can be placed in any memory location using POKE. (At least, it can be placed in any location that is physically situated in an area of RAM. If the location is in ROM it cannot be written to, even with a POKE.) The command

POKE 32768, 42

can be read as 'place the number 42 in the memory location with address 32768'. Using PEEK any memory location can be examined and, as an example, the assignment

X=PEEK (32768)

can be read as 'find what number is stored in location 32768 and then assign it to X'.

Thus PEEK can be used to examine the contents of the memory, and could be used to see how BASIC programs are stored or to examine the contents of a ROM. Because POKE can be used to change the contents of the memory it should be used with care. Poking a number indiscriminately into the area occupied by a BASIC program will change the program, thus causing what may have been a perfectly good program to behave very strangely the next time it is run. However, in the same way, POKE can be included in a program to make the program modify itself when it is run, thus opening a whole range of new applications. Programs to re-number other BASIC programs use this principle. Machine code programs can also be loaded into the memory by using POKE.

Some micros, including the PET, have memory-mapped screens.

COLUMN

	1	2	3	•	•	•	40
1	32768	32769	32770	•	•	•	32807
2	32808	32809	32810	•	•	•	32847
3	32848	32849	32850	•	•	•	32887
•	•	•	•	•	•	•	
•	•	•	•	•	•	•	
•	•	•	•	•	•	•	
25	33728	33729	33730				33767

ROW

Fig. 2.4. The PET screen has 1000 character positions. In the diagram character positions are marked with the address of the memory location to which they are mapped

28

Their screen display is produced by examining the contents of a particular area of the memory: the screen is said to be mapped to this region of memory. To give a concrete example, let us consider the PET. Its screen has 25 rows along each of which a character can occupy any one of 40 positions, giving 1000 character positions in all. At any time the display is produced by examining the memory locations with addresses from 32768 to 33767. The way in which the screen is memory-mapped is shown in *Fig. 2.4*. When a number is stored in one of these locations the character having this number as its code appears in the corresponding screen position.

The POKE command can therefore be used to generate displays on a memory-mapped screen by using it to place the appropriate numbers in the screen memory. *Fig. 2.5* illustrates the chain of events that occurs when a single POKE command is used in this way.

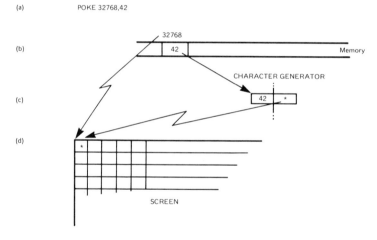

Fig. 2.5. The effect of the poking into screen memory. The POKE command (a) gives the memory contents (b). But location 32768 is mapped to the top left of the screen. The character generator (c) shows that 42 is the code for *. So the screen appears as in (d)

Summary of BASIC

This treatment of BASIC is intended to show what the language is like by describing the features it possesses, showing why it possesses them and illustrating how they are used in programs. The coverage is not complete, nor is it intended to be. Its main aims are to convey the flavour of BASIC while illustrating its capabilities.

BASIC is a language for describing such things as computations, solution methods and control procedures: its use of English words helps to make it easy to learn, but it is an artificial language and it is necessary to learn slightly new ways of thinking about problems to use it successfully.

BASIC offers a small repertoire of programming structures, although like all programming languages it offers the user the capability to construct others. It is possible to describe any computation in BASIC, but for writing lengthy programs it has definite shortcomings which result from its lack of good programming structures. As we shall see, in such cases other languages may be preferable.

Pascal

Pascal was devised by Professor Niklaus Wirth of the Federal Institute of Technology, Zurich, in 1970. He named the language after the seventeenth-century French mathematician, Blaise Pascal, whose achievements included the invention of the first calculating machine. The language was first implemented by its designer: implementations are now available for all the popular microcomputers. Wirth's main reason for developing Pascal was to provide a language for teaching programming as a systematic discipline in such a way that the principles of the discipline were clearly reflected by the language. It was based on the earlier programming language Algol 60, preserving all the desirable features of that language, but amending and extending it where necessary.

The fact that Pascal has been widely adopted not only for teaching programming but also in microprocessor system development and by users of microcomputers is a measure of its success and also an indication of the success of its designer in meeting his main aim. It was also intended that reliable and efficient implementations of the language could be developed for any computer. In this area Pascal seems not to have been quite so successful. Many of its implementations are far from compact, requiring far more storage than implementations of BASIC. Also, the implementations of the language available for micros are usually not full implementations.

That the development of programs should be a systematic discipline ought to be clear to anyone who has ever tried to write a lengthy program. The benefits of a language that permits the logical structure of a program to be expressed clearly are the production of uncomplicated, readable, self-documenting programs that can be easily checked, understood and amended.

30

To begin the description of Pascal, we give a simple Pascal program for adding two numbers together and printing the result. Alongside, the corresponding BASIC program is given for purposes of comparison.

Pascal	*BASIC*
PROGRAM ADD;	10 A=1
VAR	20 B=7
A, B, C: INTEGER;	30 C=A+B
BEGIN	40 PRINT "SUM IS", C
A:=1; B:=7; C:=A+B;	50 END
WRITELN ("SUM IS", C)	
END.	

There are many striking differences between the two programs. Perhaps the most striking is that the Pascal program has a formal framework consisting of a title, a declaration section and a section for describing the action to be taken when the program is executed. In the declaration section all the variables to be used in the computation are declared. The action part consists of all the individual actions to be taken preceded by 'BEGIN' and terminated by 'END.'.

The formal structure may be represented in the following way, where essential words are written in capital letters:

```
PROGRAM name of program;
declarations;
BEGIN
      actions
END.
```

There are no line numbers in Pascal, and there is, indeed, no concept of a line. A semicolon is used to separate each item from the next, assuming that there is one, and so a Pascal program can be laid out in any way that pleases or helps the user. Indentation has been used to highlight the form of the Pascal program given above, and it will be used subsequently to emphasise the structure of programs. This style of presentation is usually called 'pretty printing'.

The compound assignment symbol (:=) serves to remind that the instructions using it require an assignment as well as to distinguish between assignment and the equals sign in an equality relation. WRITELN causes the items in its following bracketed list to be printed out and then causes the printing position to move to a new line so that the next items to be printed will appear on the following line. Pascal also possesses a WRITE statement which simply prints the items in its associated list.

The types of variable provided by Pascal are integer, real, character and boolean. The arithmetic operations for real and integer variables are as in BASIC with two exceptions. First there is no operator for exponentiation. The second concerns the situation when one integer is divided by another. The result of this is not always an integer, and to deal with this Pascal provides the operators DIV and MOD. DIV gives the truncated integer result of the division, so that 10 DIV 3 is 3, while MOD gives the remainder: 10 MOD 3 is 1. (3 goes into 10 three times leaving the remainder 1.) A single character can be assigned to a character variable, and boolean variables take the values true and false. The standard functions provided for use with variables of these types are given in Table 2.4.

Table 2.4. Some of Pascal's standard functions

Form of function	Given by function
ABS(X)	the absolute value of X; X must be REAL or INTEGER, and the result is of the same type as X
SQR(X)	square of X; X must be REAL or INTEGER, and the result is of the same type as X
TRUNC(X)	integer part of X; X must be REAL
ROUND(X)	nearest integer to X; X must be REAL
COS(X)	cosine of X
EXP(X)	e^x
LN(X)	natural log of X
SIN(X)	sine of X
SQRT(X)	square root of X
ARCTAN(X)	inverse tan of X

For the functions COS(X), EXP(X), LN(X), SIN(X), SQRT(X), ARCTAN(X): X must be REAL or INTEGER; the result is REAL

For input, the READ statement is provided. The next short program illustrates the use of READ and assignment to variables of the different types.

```
PROGRAM ASSIGN;
VAR    NUMBER: REAL;
       I: INTEGER;
       LETTER: CHAR;
       B: BOOLEAN;
BEGIN
       READ (NUMBER);
       I:= ROUND (SQRT (NUMBER));
```

```
          LETTER:='Q';
          B:=TRUE;
          WRITELN (NUMBER, I)
END.
```

Programming structures

Pascal provides a complete range of programming structures with
which any program can be given a clear, logical structure. To start
with, any set of statements can be grouped into a block simply by
surrounding them with BEGIN and END. This is a considerable
convenience because a block can usually be placed anywhere that a
single statement can.

The conditional statement takes the form

IF condition THEN action 1 ELSE action 2

where action 1 and action 2 can be described by single statements or
by blocks of statements. A typical example is

```
IF CH='Y' THEN YCOUNT:=YCOUNT+1
ELSE YSTATE:=FALSE;
```

The following statements will read a number and cause separate
actions depending on whether it is zero, positive or negative.

```
READ(NUMBER);
IF NUMBER=0 THEN
BEGIN
          COUNT:=COUNT+1; PSTATE:=FALSE
END
ELSE      IF NUMBER>0 THEN
          PSTATE:=TRUE
          ELSE PSTATE:=FALSE;
```

The program 'shape' of the conditional statement is illustrated in
Fig. 2.6a.

When it is necessary to select one action from a fairly large number of possibilities, the continued use of IF-THEN-ELSE can be
cumbersome and can result in programs that are difficult to read.
For this kind of multiple selection Pascal provides the CASE statement: its 'shape' is shown in *Fig. 2.6b*. A typical CASE statement,
which allows one of four possible actions to be selected depending on
the value of the integer variable I when the statement is executed, is:

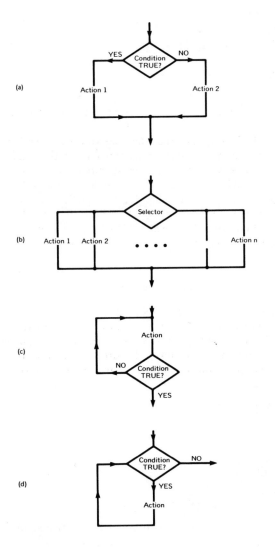

Fig. 2.6. Programming 'shapes' provided by Pascal (a) IF condition THEN action1 ELSE action2 (b) CASE (c) REPEAT action UNTIL condition (d) WHILE condition DO action

34

```
CASE I   OF
    1:   Y:=SIN(X);
    2:   Y:=COS(X);
    3:   Y:=LN(X);
    4:   Y:=EXP(X)
END
```

when I is 1 only the statement labelled 1 is selected, and so on for the other cases.

Pascal supports three features for handling repetition. When the number of repetitions required is known in advance there is a FOR statement similar to the one in BASIC. It has the form

```
FOR I:=1 TO 20 DO
```

and controls the next instruction or block of instructions. There is a REPEAT-UNTIL statement which allows a group of instructions to be executed repeatedly until a specified condition becomes true. It has the general form

```
REPEAT
    statements
UNTIL condition;
```

Its 'shape' is shown in *Fig. 2.6c*. The next program is intended to illustrate the use of this form of repetition by reading numbers and counting them until a zero is read. Thus the program counts the data items that it reads, up to and including the terminating zero.

```
PROGRAM COUNT;
    VAR DATA, COUNT: INTEGER;
BEGIN
    COUNT:=0;
    REPEAT
        READ (DATA);
        COUNT:=COUNT+1
    UNTIL DATA=0;
    WRITELN ('DATA COUNT IS', COUNT)
END.
```

Pascal can also support repetition while some condition is true. The form of this statement is

```
WHILE condition DO
    block;
```

Its 'shape' is given in *Fig. 2.6d*. To illustrate the use of this, the next short program reads two numbers and prints out their difference while the first number is bigger than the second.

```
PROGRAM PAIR;
   VAR A, B, C: REAL;
BEGIN
   WRITELN ('ENTER NUMBERS');
   READ (A, B);
   WHILE A>B DO
     BEGIN
        C:=A−B;
        WRITELN (C);
        WRITELN ('ENTER NUMBERS');
        READ (A, B)
     END
END.
```

Procedures

In Pascal the sub-program is the procedure. A procedure must be declared before it can be used and this is done by giving the complete procedure definition: procedure declarations should be placed immediately after the variable declarations. A procedure is called simply by giving its name.

The following Pascal program includes a procedure to generate a box composed of asterisks. The program is designed to produce the same output as one of the BASIC programs given previously.

```
PROGRAM BOXES;
PROCEDURE STARBOX:
BEGIN
   WRITELN ('******');
   WRITELN ('*    *');
   WRITELN ('******')
END;
BEGIN
   STARBOX;
   WRITELN ('NANCY');
   STARBOX;
   WRITELN ('BEN');
   STARBOX
END.
```

The procedure in this program is the simplest kind possible, causing exactly the same computation each time it is called. This may not always be what is required of a procedure, and it is possible to write procedures that accept values from t`.e calling program and which pass results back to it. One advantage of using simple procedures is

36

that, by choosing suitable names for them, programs can be made extremely easy to read and to understand. The meaning of a program fragment such as

```
REPEAT
  FETCHINSTRUCTION;
  DECODE;
  EXECUTE
UNTIL INSTRUCTION='END'
```

is entirely obvious.

To illustrate a more general procedure, consider writing a procedure to generate a starbox with M stars along its horizontal sides and N along the vertical sides. A procedure for this could be:

```
PROCEDURE STARBOX2(M,N:INTEGER);
VAR I,J,K: INTEGER;
BEGIN
  FOR I:=1 TO M DO
    WRITE('*');
  WRITELN;
  FOR J:=1 TO N-2 DO
    BEGIN
        WRITE('*');
        FOR K:=1 TO M-2 DO
            WRITE(' ');
        WRITE('*');
        WRITELN;
    END;
  FOR I:=1 TO M DO
    WRITE('*');
  WRITELN
END;
```

The procedure could be called, for example, by STARBOX2 (8,4). The example shows that the form of a procedure is the same as that of a program.

Structuring data

Pascal provides a particularly rich variety of facilities for structuring data. It is possible to have arrays of all the data types; the file is supported as a data type, and if none of these satisfies the user's requirements then Pascal permits the user to create his own data types.

Any set of data items can be grouped together to form a record which can be defined as a new data type; then variables of this type can be declared and subsequently manipulated as single items. To give an example of this, in a three-dimensional graphics system it would undoubtedly be convenient to manipulate a point as a single item rather than having to deal with its three coordinates individually. For this purpose a new data type for points could be created consisting of a record containing the three coordinates. The following program fragment shows how to define the new data type, where to place the definition and how to make an assignment to a component of a record.

```
PROGRAM GRAPHICS;
  TYPE POINT=RECORD
                    X, Y, Z: REAL
            END;
  VAR CORNER, TOP: POINT;
BEGIN
  CORNER.X:=7.6;
  TOP.X:=21.7;
  CORNER.Y:=5.1;
    .
    .
    .
```

The last program in this section is a complete one which creates a variable especially for recording details of a house, permits these details to be entered and creates a file containing the details of a series of houses. In this way the program can create a database. The program illustrates a number of the features that have already been mentioned, and also shows how easy it is to handle files in Pascal. The program is:

```
PROGRAM HOUSEFILE (G);
TYPE HOUSE=RECORD
               NUMBER: INTEGER;
               NAME: PACKED ARRAY [1:20] OF CHAR;
               LENGTH, WIDTH: REAL
          END;
VAR H: HOUSE;
    G: FILE OF HOUSE;
BEGIN
  REWRITE (G);
  WRITELN ('ENTER NUMBER');
  READ (H. NUMBER);
  WHILE H. NUMBER<>0 DO
    BEGIN
```

```
      WRITELN ('ENTER NAME');
      GETLN;
      READ (H.NAME);
      WRITELN ('ENTER LENGTH');
      READ (H.LENGTH);
      WRITELN ('ENTER WIDTH');
      READ (H.WIDTH);
      G ↑ :=H;
      PUT (G);
      WRITELN ('ENTER NUMBER');
      READ (NUMBER)
    END;
    RESET (G);
  END.
```

The record of type HOUSE consists of an integer to hold the number of the house, a string of 20 characters for its name and two reals for its length and width. However, when written to a file, a house variable is handled as a single item.

The declaration of G as a FILE OF HOUSE means that it is a file to which variables of type HOUSE can be written. REWRITE(G) ensures that the file is empty before any records are written to it. Pascal maintains a 'buffer variable' for communication between a program and a file: when the file is called G the buffer variable is denoted by G ↑ . The statement G ↑ :=H sets the buffer variable to the current house variable, and PUT(G) then puts it in the file.

Summary of Pascal

This informal introduction to Pascal is intended to give an appreciation of the features and capabilities of the language. As with BASIC, it is not a complete description. Pascal is a general-purpose language in which programs can be developed in a systematic way: when a program is written for a specific task it can be given a logical structure which is the same as that of the task. This helps in the initial design of the program as well as being a considerable help in amending and maintaining it.

Pascal provides a wide repertoire of programming structures and permits data types to be defined as required. Consequently, the programmer is provided with all the features necessary to give his programs a logical structure and also with the capability to design his own data structures if those supplied as standards by Pascal do not meet his needs. In this way there is no need to resort to artificial or idiosyncratic ways of designing programs and handling data.

The disciplines imposed by Pascal, such as requiring the programmer to declare each variable and to say how it will be used, should be seen as beneficial because by allowing systematic program development they cause many of the more common programming errors to be avoided automatically.

Structured programming

A talented singer can sing a song so that each line clearly follows the next and the whole song is shaped into a complete performance. In the same way a good programmer can take a task and write a program that has a suitable logical structure. But just as some songs are better vehicles than others for singers, so some programming languages permit the expression of an intended structure for a program better than others.

One systematic way to develop a program is to start with the task for which a program is to be written, to refine the task into sub-tasks, and to continually refine the sub-tasks into smaller tasks until all the end sub-tasks become sufficiently small. The sub-tasks can be considered small enough when a program module can easily be written for each one. The refinement process is illustrated schematically in *Fig. 2.7.*

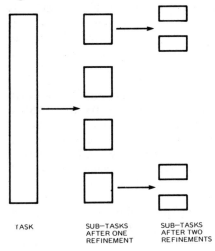

TASK   SUB—TASKS   SUB—TASKS
           AFTER ONE   AFTER TWO
           REFINEMENT   REFINEMENTS

Fig. 2.7. Schematic representation of the continuous refinement of a task into sub-tasks

40

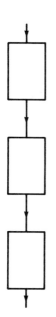

Fig. 2.8.   The linkage of modules each with a single entry and exit point

Each sub-task, and therefore each program module, should have only one entry point and one exit point as illustrated in *Fig. 2.8*. This makes it as easy as possible to link all the modules together to make the complete program. Also, it makes it easy to amend the program by removing and replacing a module. The decision as to whether a module should be written as, say, a procedure or a block using the appropriate programming 'shape' can be taken in the light of the overall structure. It can be observed from *Fig. 2.6* that all the Pascal programming 'shapes' are appropriate to this strategy because they all have a single input point and output point. If this so-called 'top-down' design procedure can be followed then the structure of the program will be the same as that of the task.

In a book on programming languages the following points must be made rather strongly. First, the refinement process must be carried out in a logical way without imposing any unnecessary restrictions, particularly the restrictions that a programming language might require. Second, the language in which the program is to be written need not be decided on until the refinement is complete. After the refinement it may well become clear that one language is more suitable than others.

A comparison of BASIC and Pascal

In this section BASIC and Pascal are compared according to several different criteria. The comparison is not intended to show that one is a better language than the other, but to reveal the ways in which one may be more suitable than the other in a particular application.

1. *Ease of learning.* BASIC is easier to learn than Pascal because there is less formality: there are fewer ideas and conventions to master before starting to write programs. However, it is doubtful whether it is easier to *learn to write good programs* in BASIC than in Pascal because the formalities of Pascal are an aid to developing good programs.
2. *Discipline.* Whereas BASIC imposes practically no discipline at all, Pascal insists that all programs have the same formal framework and that all variables, procedures, etc. are declared before they are used. It is possible to write badly structured programs in BASIC and in Pascal, but the discipline of Pascal provides the programmer wanting to write well-structured programs with every assistance.
3. *Structure.* Pascal provides all the programming features necessary to write well-structured programs perhaps by following the top-down method of program design. The BASIC programmer is not so well provided with programming constructs. When using top-down design the problem is that it is difficult, and sometimes impossible, to reduce program modules with a single entry and exit *that can be written in BASIC* to a reasonable size.
4. *Readability.* Good Pascal programs can be readable to the point that they are self-documenting. Good program structure and well-chosen names for variables and procedures all help to make this possible. With the best will in the world long BASIC programs can be difficult to read and therefore to understand.
5. *Safety.* Pascal is a safe language in the sense that it prevents the programmer from making many of the more common errors merely by the disciplines that it imposes. By contrast, BASIC lets the programmer make any mistakes he can. Two examples should serve to illustrate the point.

In a lengthy BASIC program a variable named X, say, may have been used to hold a result for later use. However, towards the end of the program, needing a new variable for some purpose, the programmer can decide to call it X. (It has to be called something!) He may subsequently decide to recall the earlier result that was carefully stored in X, forgetting that by using X for something else that result has been replaced. Consequently the program will produce faulty results. The Pascal programmer *can* do exactly the same thing but, since all variables are declared before they are used, when a new variable name is required a list exists in the program of all the variable names used to that point.

The second example concerns sub-programs. In BASIC a subroutine appears exactly like a section of program: it has no formal heading to mark its beginning. Consequently when a program is being executed it is possible to get into a subroutine by accident and without actually calling it. In Pascal, since procedures must be declared and are then called by giving their names, a procedure cannot be executed by accident.

These points are not criticisms of BASIC, but simply illustrations of how the careless use of BASIC can give unexpected and faulty results.

Self-test questions

1. Write BASIC assignments as follows:
   (a) to assign the product of A, B and C to X;
   (b) to assign the sum of A^2 and B^2 to W;
   (c) to assign the difference of X and Y divided by 16 to Q.

2. Write the assignments described in question 1 in Pascal.

3. Draw a diagram to represent the way the variables and the values assigned to them are held in memory when the following program is run. What results are printed by the program?

```
 10   A=1
 20   B=2
 30   C=A+B
 40   D=A+3*B+2
 50   Z=D/C
 60   PRINT Z
 70   D=D+C
 80   D=D/C
 90   PRINT D
100   END
```

4. Write a BASIC program to accept data and process it in the following way:
   (a) assign the values 0 and 1 to A and B;
   (b) print an appropriate caption;
   (c) accept a value for X;
   (d) assign the sum of B and X to A;
   (e) assign the difference of A and X to B;

(f)　print A and B;

(g)　return to step (c) and continue unless the last number accepted was zero.

5. Write a program for the task described in question 4 in Pascal.

6. Write a program in BASIC to convert a number of minutes expressed in decimal form to minutes and seconds. The program should accept the decimal number and if, for example, it is given 3.25 it should print
   THE NUMBER OF MINUTES IS 3
   THE NUMBER OF SECONDS IS 15

7. Explain the computations described by the following BASIC programs and the results they give.

(a)
```
10  T=0.1
20  FOR J=0 TO 100
30  W=T*J
40  Y=EXP(-W)*SIN(2*W)
50  PRINT Y
60  NEXT J
70  END
```

(b)
```
10  J=1
20  PRINT "ENTER AN INTEGER"
30  INPUT N
40  FOR I=1 TO N
50  J=J*I
60  NEXT I
70  PRINT J
80  END
```

(c)
```
10   X$="1234567890"
20   A$=""
30   L=LEN(X$)
40   IF L=0 THEN GOTO 90
50   B$=RIGHT$ (X$, 2)
60   X$=LEFT$ (X$, L-2)
70   A$=A$+B$
80   GOTO 30
90   PRINT A$
100  END
```

8. Devise Pascal data structures suitable for the following applications:

(a) A three-dimensional computer graphics system which,

besides handling POINTS, must deal with LINES, REC-
TANGLES, CIRCLES and POLYGONS.

(b) Dealing with circuits that are known to contain not more
than two circuit elements.

3

Other languages for microcomputers

This chapter deals with languages other than BASIC and Pascal that are available for microcomputers. Some of the languages described are becoming increasingly widely used, particularly in areas for which they have been found especially suitable. The aims of the treatment of each language are to indicate why the language exists and what it is intended for, to illustrate what the language is like by describing some of its features and constructs, and to show what it is like to use the language by giving some typical programs and program fragments.

COMAL

The fundamental reason for the existence of COMAL is much more clear-cut and easy to find than it is for most of the languages covered in this book. COMAL (COMmon Algorithmic Language) exists because of the dissatisfaction of the Danish educationalist Borge Christensen with Microsoft BASIC and all the similar BASICs available for microcomputers.

Christensen became convinced that BASIC was generally unsuitable for teaching good programming practice in the school environment. When using microcomputers in school he wanted to retain the simplicity of BASIC, which makes it so easy to learn, but he felt very strongly that BASIC was not a satisfactory vehicle for writing well-structured programs. As a result, he developed a language to meet his own requirements. He did this by observing the needs and difficulties of his own students, and introducing facilities that he thought would fulfil their needs and help them to overcome their problems. He found his students responsive to his innovations, readily seeing the point of them, and as a result accepting them.

The new features of COMAL are rather close to the control structures of Pascal, so that COMAL can be seen as a hybrid of BASIC and Pascal which possesses many of the best properties of both languages. This hybrid can, and should, benefit not only students learning a language for the first time, but also any programmer seeking a language that remains reasonably simple while permitting the production of well-structured programs. Christensen has stated that programs using COMAL to advantage can be developed more quickly than with BASIC, and that they can be maintained much more easily.

In the educational environment, the specific advantages of COMAL as a hybrid of BASIC and Pascal are that it is easy to learn, so that the student can progress from scratch very quickly, and that it also provides a bridge to Pascal which is the major computing language used in most university and polytechnic degree courses in computing.

COMAL is widely used on microcomputers in many countries, including Denmark and Germany. The education ministries of both Denmark and Ireland have opted for COMAL as the universal language for use in their secondary schools.

The features of COMAL

A brief description of COMAL is given in this section with the aims of giving a flavour of the language and of showing how it combines features of BASIC and Pascal.

Variable names can be up to 16 characters long and must start with a letter. This permits variables to be given names that are indicative of their function, and can allow programs to be much more readable than their BASIC counterparts. The assignment symbol is as in Pascal, so that typical simple assignments are

TEAMNUMBER:=10
STATUS$:= "MARRIED"

These assignments are almost as readable as English. The use of the Pascal assignment symbol removes the apparent ambiguity of a BASIC statement such as

IF C=10 THEN C=0.9*C

This could be written in COMAL as

IF COST=10 THEN COST:=0.9*COST

which shows clearly that the instruction contains both a test for equality and an assignment.

COMAL provides both TRUE and FALSE as predefined constants (they are equivalent to 1 and 0 respectively). They permit such suggestive assignments as

FINISHED:=TRUE

The programming structures possessed by the language include the conditional instruction in the form IF-THEN-ELSE, selection by CASE OF, and repetitions controlled by any of REPEAT-UNTIL, FOR-DO and WHILE-DO. The language has an inbuilt 'pretty printing' feature which causes these features to be indented automatically when a program is listed. This makes programs much easier to read, and, as importantly, it provides an extremely useful aid in debugging programs since incorrectly written structures can be spotted with ease simply by examining the indentation arrangement. The following program fragment illustrates the way that a conditional statement appears with the aid of pretty printing.

```
IF RESPONSE$="YES" THEN
    PRINT "ENTER CODE FOR NEXT JOB"
    INPUT JOBCODE
ELSE
    PRINT "END OF PROGRAM"
    FINISHED:=TRUE
ENDIF
```

The way in which ENDIF terminates an instruction starting with IF is typical of COMAL: to give another example, the end of the group of instructions controlled by WHILE-DO is indicated by ENDWHILE. This style of termination originated with Algol 68 where, typically, the terminator for IF is FI.

The sub-program in COMAL is the procedure rather than the subroutine of BASIC. Procedures can be given names that are indicative of their purposes; this makes programs much more readable since COMAL's EXEC DATASEARCH cannot avoid being more informative than BASIC's GOSUB 8000. A procedure called INITIALISE is declared by

```
PROC INITIALISE
    SUM:=0
    PRODUCT:=1
    ITEMS:=0
    MEAN:=0
ENDPROC
```

This procedure is executed by the statement

EXEC INITIALISE

COMAL supports recursion, so that, in particular, a procedure may call itself. The primary data structure provided is the array. A wide range of commands is available, including those that are present in BASIC such as RUN, LIST and SAVE, but with additional ones including automatic line number generation and line renumbering.

A COMAL program

The following program listing is intended to display a fairly typical COMAL program, which contains many of the features already described. It also shows how COMAL combines the attributes of BASIC and Pascal in its own distinctive blend.

```
010   FINISHED:=FALSE; TOTAL:=0; CORRECT:=0
020   REPEAT
030      FOR K:=1 TO 4 DO PRINT
040      PRINT "ENTER CODES AS FOLLOWS"
050      PRINT "1 FOR ADDITION"
060      PRINT "2 FOR SUBTRACTION"
070      PRINT "3 FOR MULTIPLICATION"
080      PRINT "4 FOR DIVISION"
090      PRINT "5 TO STOP"
100      INPUT    "ENTER    CODE    FOR    PROBLEM
         REQUIRED": TYPE
110      CASE TYPE OF
120      WHEN 1
130         EXEC ADD
140         EXEC RECORD
150      WHEN 2
160         EXEC SUBTRACT
170         EXEC RECORD
180      WHEN 3
  .
  .
  .
240      WHEN 5
250         FINISHED:=TRUE
260      OTHERWISE
270         PRINT "NO SUCH COMMAND"
280      ENDCASE
290   UNTIL FINISHED
300   PROC ADD
310      N1:=RND(20,100); N2:=RND(2,10)
320      RESULT:=N1+N2
```

```
330    SIGN$:="+"
340  ENDPROC ADD
350  PROC RECORD
360    PRINT "GIVE THE VALUE OF"
370    PRINT N1:SIGN$: N2
380    INPUT ANSWER
390    TOTAL:=TOTAL+1
400    IF    ANSWER=RESULT    THEN    CORRECT:=
       CORRECT+1
410  ENDPROC RECORD
```

This skeleton program should be sufficiently easy to read to convey
that it is a mathematical problem drill program, with a menu of
arithmetic test problems and a means of selecting problems that
include randomly generated numbers. The procedures for generating subtraction, multiplication and division problems are not given,
but they will be similar to the procedure ADD. The procedure
RECORD displays the problems, accepts an answer and then keeps
a record of the user's successes. It ought, perhaps, to be rather fuller
in that it should produce remarks appropriate to the answers that
are given and should keep a record of success for each of the various
types of problem. The modifications to the program to make it do
these things are, however, straightforward.

Implementations of COMAL

COMAL has been implemented for several microcomputers. The
first implementation available in this country was for the PET (it
was released by Commodore as public-domain software) and
Christensen was involved in its development. The most recent version of COMAL is known as COMAL-80 and this is now available
for the PET. It is also available on a Danish machine which is mar-
keted in this country under the name 'Piccolo'.

COMAL implementations require rather a large amount of store,
typically in excess of 20K, so that if they have to be loaded into
RAM, as they do on the PET, they leave not too much memory
available for storing COMAL programs.

FORTRAN

FORTRAN was the first high-level language: it was developed by
IBM and first released in 1957. Its name is a contraction of FOR-

mula TRANslation, and this gives a good indication of the aims of the language which were, as stated in the first FORTRAN manual, to provide a language capable of expressing any problem in numerical computation, particularly problems involving large sets of formulae and many variables. It was admitted that FORTRAN might not be ideal for problems outside the numerical area and, indeed, the major areas of application have been in scientific and engineering problem-solving. The language has, however, also been successfully applied in other problem areas.

The original version of FORTRAN was developed to run on a particular machine—the IBM 704—and was conceived in the light of the characteristics of that machine. Some of the aspects of FORTRAN therefore have their origins in the form of a particular computer, and the design of the language is not totally logical but reflects what could conveniently be achieved on that machine. This is in stark contrast to the language Algol 60, which was contemporary with FORTRAN and which is a logically structured and formally defined language (see Appendix 1).

The importance of FORTRAN as the first of the high-level languages was that it provided an alternative to assembly code that offered programmers relief from the tyranny of detail imposed by the latter. Since its introduction it has evolved through many versions, including FORTRAN II, FORTRAN IV and FORTRAN 77. It was the first language ever to be standardised by a national standards body (FORTRAN IV was enshrined in a standard form by the American National Standards Institute). During its evolution FORTRAN has acquired many additions, some of which are intended to make it suitable for non-numeric computations, but its original core has remained. Incidentally, BASIC is derived from FORTRAN II.

Since FORTRAN led the way as the first high-level computer language, but has subsequently been overtaken by many more modern languages, it may seem surprising that it has survived so strongly. However, the number of programmers who have learnt it, the existence of large amounts of software written in it and the existence of many applications libraries, including the graphics package GINO-F, written in FORTRAN, all combine to ensure that FORTRAN is, and will continue to be, widely used.

The FORTRAN instruction repertoire

The brief account of FORTRAN given here relates to standard FORTRAN IV. Because FORTRAN programs were originally presented punched on cards to computers FORTRAN statements have to be prepared in a particular format, even when entered from a keyboard, which reflects the arrangement of a punch card. Statements must begin in column 7, while columns 1 to 5 are reserved for statement numbers. A 'C' in the first column indicates that the line is a comment, presumably to aid in the documentation of the program, and is to be ignored when the FORTRAN program is translated. When there is any entry in column 6 this indicates that the line is a continuation of the previous one: in this way FORTRAN can deal with statements that are too long to fit on one line. This 'card image' is illustrated in *Fig. 3.1*.

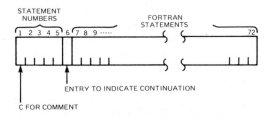

Fig. 3.1. FORTRAN card image

The names of variables can be up to six characters long; they must begin with a letter, but subsequent characters can be letters or numbers. By default, names that begin with any letter from I to N inclusive indicate integer variables, and anything else is the name of a real variable. Thus the assignment

FIVE=5.0

assigns a real value to a real variable, but

ITWO=2

assigns an integer value to an integer variable. Real numbers are stored in floating-point form as numbers from 0.1 up to, but not including, 1.0, multiplied by a power of ten as appropriate. Other kinds of variables can be declared and used including logical, complex and double-precision. The last are used when high accuracy is needed in the results of numerical calculations. Variables of these kinds can be declared with statements such as

LOGICAL L1, L2
COMPLEX Z1, Z2
DOUBLE PRECISION DX

After these declarations have been made, assignments such as the following can be given

L1=.FALSE.
Z1=CMPLX(2.0, 4.0)
L2=K.EQ.2

In these, the complex number $2 +j4$ is assigned to Z1, and L2 is assigned the logical value true or false according as the value currently assigned to K is 2 or not.

FORTRAN supplies the functions that are typically available on a scientific calculator, plus a few more, and these include the logarithmic, exponential, sine, cosine and absolute value functions. There are also some functions which accept complex numbers and produce complex-valued results.

The keywords of FORTRAN can be summarised to outline the features possessed by the language. They include DIMENSION for declaring an array, IF in the conditional statement, DO-CONTINUE to demarcate a group of statements to be executed repeatedly, READ and WRITE for input and output, FORMAT statements to accompany READ and WRITE and indicate the form in which the input should be presented and the output is to be produced, a GOTO statement and, finally, FUNCTION and SUB-ROUTINE which indicate the two types of sub-programs supported by the language.

A typical FORTRAN program

Since FORTRAN was primarily intended for scientific and engineering computations, in this section a FORTRAN program is presented for solving a typical problem in numerical analysis, namely, finding the solution of an equation.

The Newton-Raphson method is a well-known technique for solving an equation such as

$$\sin x = x + 1$$

This equation is not at all easy to solve by conventional methods, but its solution can be found using the Newton-Raphson method, as can that of any equation involving a single unknown, x.

Any equation in one unknown can be written as

$$f(x) = 0$$

In this form, the equation given above becomes

$$\sin x - x - 1 = 0$$

When the equation is expressed in this way, its solution can be found approximately by the graphical method of plotting the curves $y=f(x)$ and $y=0$ (which is the x-axis) and finding the value of x, $x=x_{app}$, say, at which they cross. At this value of x, $f(x)$ is equal to zero and so the equation is satisfied. The solution obtained in this way is necessarily approximate however, because a graph can only be read to a certain accuracy. *Fig. 3.2* shows the parts of the curves $y=\sin x-x-1$ and $y=0$ in the region in which they intersect.

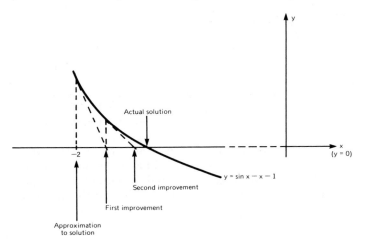

Fig. 3.2. Newton-Raphson method for solving $\sin x-x-1=0$

This provides a starting point for explaining the Newton-Raphson method, which works by taking an approximate solution, obtained graphically or otherwise, and improves it to any required accuracy. The method, again illustrated in *Fig. 3.2*, is to draw the tangent to the curve $y=f(x)$ at $x=x_{app}$ and to extend the tangent until it cuts the x-axis, taking the value of x at which this occurs as an improved approximation to the solution, $x=x_{imp}$. The procedure can be repeated as often as necessary to give a desired accuracy by taking the improved approximation, calling it x_{app} and then calculating a new x_{imp} from it.

The Newton-Raphson formula describing this procedure is, in its general form

$$x_{imp}=x_{app}-f(x_{app})/f'(x_{app})$$

Now consider the precisely defined problem of using the Newton-Raphson method to improve the approximate value of -2.0 for the solution of

54

$$\sin x - x - 1 = 0$$

until it is accurate to 5 decimal places. In this case the Newton-Raphson formula becomes

$$x_{imp} = (x_{app} \cos x_{app} - \sin x_{app} + 1)/(\cos x_{app} - 1)$$

and a flowchart on which a program to solve the problem can be based is given in *Fig. 3.3.* The resulting FORTRAN program is listed below.

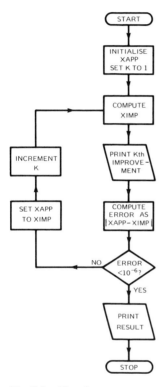

Fig. 3.3. Flowchart

```
        XAPP=-2.0
        K=1
  5     XIMP=(XAPP*COS(XAPP)-SIN(XAPP)+1.0)/
        (COS(XAPP)-1.0)
        WRITE(5, 100) K, XIMP
        ERROR=ABS(XIMP-XAPP)
```

```
        IF (ERROR.LT. 1.0E−6) GOTO 6
        K=K+1
        XAPP=XIMP
        GOTO 5
6       WRITE(5, 101) XIMP
100     FORMAT(1X, 'APPROXIMATION    NUMBER',    I3,
        ' IS', F12.6)
101     FORMAT(1X, 'THE RESULT IS', F12.5)
        STOP
        END
```

The successive approximations and result given by this program are:

```
APPROXIMATION NUMBER 1 IS −1.935951
APPROXIMATION NUMBER 2 IS −1.934564
APPROXIMATION NUMBER 3 IS −1.934563
APPROXIMATION NUMBER 4 IS −1.934563
THE RESULT IS     −1.93456
```

In the two WRITE statements, the bracketed pair of numbers gives a channel number and the number of the associated FORMAT statement. Channel 5 is usually the channel to the default display device. The FORMAT statements give the precise form in which the WRITE statements should present their output.

Implementations of FORTRAN

FORTRAN is available for most of the popular microcomputers. It is available under CP/M so that it can be run on all CP/M machines. Other implementations that are available include a version for the Research Machines 380Z, a cassette-based version for the Sharp MZ80K, FORTRAN 77 for the Apple and Microsoft FORTRAN IV for the Tandy TRS80.

Lisp

The purpose of Lisp is LISt Processing. Processing lists may not seem to be a sufficiently common activity to require a special language, but the fact is that a list is a particularly general data structure, and with its aid many types of problems can be tackled in a rather natural way. As an example of a familiar situation where the underlying structure can be regarded as a list, words can be seen as lists of letters and sentences as lists of words. A robot which can automatically move freely within its environment provides an illustration of an application where a list can be used to advantage; by maintaining a list of obstacles and their locations, the robot can check its list before making a movement to ensure that it is not about to bump into something. In fact the list is a useful way of keeping any collection of data that needs to be searched or sorted with any regularity.

Because Lisp can deal with lists of any kind of items, it permits non-numeric computations to be described and performed, and in particular it provides a tool for symbol manipulation. Lisp was developed by Professor John McCarthy and his students at the Massachusetts Institute of Technology at the beginning of the 1960s. Their original aim was to develop a programming system called the Advice Taker which would be able to handle both facts and commands, using the facts in a common-sense way to help in interpreting and carrying out the commands. Workers in other areas, particularly those engaged in Artificial Intelligence (AI) work, soon realised that McCarthy's language provided the means of manipulating symbols that they were seeking. Symbol manipulation is the requirement that is common to many areas of investigation that are part of AI, including generalised problem solving, pattern recognition, theorem proving, computational linguistics and algebraic manipulation. As a result Lisp has become the most widely used language in AI.

To achieve its original aims, Lisp was developed as a language for defining and transforming functions. It is a functional language in the sense that it works by applying functions to inputs and delivering the result as output. In a functional language, program structure is controlled essentially by the way in which a complex function is composed of simpler functions. The component functions in Lisp are broadly equivalent to the procedures and subroutines of other languages.

Lisp has had a reputation for being difficult to learn, and several books have made it appear so. The appearance of some good books on Lisp (see Appendix 2) has helped to remedy this situation by revealing that Lisp is a fundamentally simple, elegant and powerful language. The concepts embodied in the language are intellectually appealing and they can take the train of thought of the user into regions that may not otherwise have been accessible.

Lists and simple programs

A list of the four items A, B, C and D is written in Lisp as

(A B C D)

Fig. 3.4. The list (A B C D)

It can be represented diagrammatically as shown in *Fig. 3.4*, which is intended to indicate that each item in the list is stored with a pointer to the next item. The pointer usually takes the form of the address of the location containing the next item. Thus, in a typical implementation, each item in a list is stored with the address of the next item. The items of a list can be either atoms (elementary data) or lists: the following list of three items gives the name and age of each of three people:

((SMITH 18) (JONES 21) (THOMPSON 33))

The power of the list as a representation is well illustrated by using a list to represent the chess position illustrated in *Fig. 3.5*. Each piece on the board is represented by a list giving its type, colour and position, and the overall position is represented by a list of these lists. The list representing the position is:

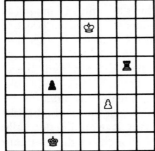

Fig. 3.5. Chess position

All Lisp programs take the form of a list: the first item in the list is a function and the remaining items are arguments (or inputs) for the function. When presented with a program Lisp deals with it by applying these three steps:

58

i. evaluate the arguments,
ii. apply the function to the evaluated arguments, and
iii. output the result that is obtained.

Thus, the program

(PLUS 7 2)

delivers the result 9 because numbers evaluate to themselves. However, if values are assigned to A and B by

(SET 'A 2)
(SET 'B 3)

then

(TIMES A B)

delivers the result 6, and the three steps that are applied in the course of dealing with any Lisp program have been brought fully into use. The quote symbol (') used with the SET function has the purpose of *preventing* evaluation when used there and elsewhere. The purpose of the first use of SET given above is to set A to 2 and not to set the *value* of A to 2.

When values have been assigned to P, Q and R the value of the expression P+Q*R can be obtained from the program

(PLUS P (TIMES Q R))

In expressions of this kind the order in which the operations are to be evaluated must be determined by the programmer. Lisp does not provide an automatic order of precedence for arithmetic operations in the way that scientific programming languages do.

Lisp provides many functions besides PLUS and TIMES. Since the language is not primarily for numerical applications the functions for non-numerical application such as the standard list processing functions CAR, CDR and CONS are more typical than the numerical ones. With these functions lists of items of any kind can be examined, dissected and constructed.

The function CAR applied to a list delivers the first item of the list. Applying CDR to a list delivers the list without its first item. Thus, after a list of items has been assigned to L by

(SET 'L '(ASH OAK ELM LIME))

the program

(CAR L)

delivers ASH, while the result of

(CDR L)

is (OAK ELM LIME). The second item in the list can be obtained by

(CAR (CDR L))

With CAR and CDR any item in a list can be obtained. While CAR and CDR permit lists to be taken apart, CONS allows lists to be constructed. The arguments for CONS are an item and a list, and the effect of this function is to add the item to the beginning of the list. In this way, the result of

(CONS 'PINE L)

is the list (PINE ASH OAK ELM LIME).

User-defined functions

Lisp permits its users to define their own functions in case the functions that it provides do not meet their requirements. For this purpose Lisp provides a function for defining other functions. To illustrate its use, consider the function which increases the value of its argument by one and which can be expressed mathematically as

$add1(x)=x+1$

This function can be defined in Lisp by

(DEFINE (ADD1 X) (PLUS X 1))

Once it has been defined this function can be used in the same way as any other Lisp function and

(ADD1 3)

gives the result 4.

Recursion

A function whose definition partly involves itself is called recursive. Powerful functions can be constructed by combining other functions, but with recursion a function is built up by using itself as a building block. In this way functions can be developed that are remarkably short and compact for the computation that they describe. They also tend to be rather elegant.

Before starting to define recursive functions in Lisp it is necessary to introduce one or two more of Lisp's functions. The function NULL is applied to a list. If the list is null, that is, if the list contains no items, then the function NULL is true (T), otherwise it is false. Thus, after

(SET 'M '(MERLIN NIMUE))

the result of

(NULL M)

is false, whereas

(NULL '( ))

is always true and always gives T.

The conditional function of Lisp is COND. It takes the form

(COND   (test1   result1)
         (test2   result2)
              . . . . .
         (testn   resultn)   )

When it is evaluated, the tests are made successively and the result delivered is that which corresponds to the first test that is found to be true. It corresponds to the perhaps more familiar structure

IF test1 THEN result1 ELSE IF test2 THEN result2 ELSE
IF test3 THEN . . . .

The following conditional function gives the result zero if the list assigned to M is null, 1 if it contains one item and 2 otherwise.

(COND   ((NULL   M)   0)
         ((NULL   (CDR   M))   1)
         (T   2))

Note that one of the tests will always succeed because the final test, T, is always true.

It is now possible, with the background acquired, to define a recursive function which takes a list as its argument and finds the number of items in the list. The idea of the function is that the number of items in a list can be found in this way:

IF the list is null THEN the number of items is zero
ELSE the number of items is one (the first item)
    plus the number of items in the rest of the list.

The function is defined by

(DEFINE   (LENGTH L)
          (COND ((NULL L)   0)
                (T (PLUS 1 (LENGTH(CDR L)))))
                                                   ))

or, using a previously defined function, by

```
(DEFINE (LENGTH L)
        (COND ((NULL L)    0)
              (T (ADD1 (LENGTH (CDR L)))))
                                         ))
```

A similar recursive function which, when applied to a list of numeric atoms, gives the sum of all the atoms in the list is defined by

```
(DEFINE (SUM L)
        (COND ((NULL L)    0)
              (T (PLUS (CAR L) (SUM (CDR L)))))
                                              ))
```

Having defined these functions, after

```
(SET 'M '(5 4 3 2 1))
```

the program

```
(LENGTH M)
```

gives the result 5, while

```
(SUM M)
```

delivers 15.

Implementations of Lisp

Implementations of Lisp are not as readily available as are those of, for example, Pascal and FORTRAN. Among those available, Commodore provide a version for the PET, there is a version for the Apple and Acorn supply a 6 Kbyte Lisp interpreter for the Atom. An implementation for 6800-based systems has been written by van der Wateren and is published in *Dr Dobbs' Journal*, number 28, pages 24–5.

APL

APL was devised by Kenneth Iverson who described it in his book *A Programming Language*, published by Wiley in 1962. The title of the book gives the language its name. Iverson's original motivation for inventing the language was not so much to provide a programming language as to devise a notation in which algorithms could be expressed precisely, and also one in which the behaviour of hardware could be described exactly. APL has been used successfully to describe computer hardware in a formal way, and also to describe the semantics, or meaning, of a programming language by providing a notation in which the effects of its instructions can be given exactly. Because of its use in applications such as these, it has been argued that APL is a system of *notation* rather than a programming language. However, APL is undoubtedly a programming language as well: it has been implemented for many machines and has found favour with programmers for many, varied applications. It was first implemented by IBM in a version known as APL/360 in the middle 1960s and it was made generally available by the end of that decade. Other implementations have followed, including some for micro-computers.

As a programming language, APL is intended for describing procedures concerned with information processing. It can deal with either numerical or textual information. The handling of arrays, such as vectors, strings and matrices is straightforward because they can all be treated as single items. This ability has led to the adoption of the language for purposes such as business planning, management and engineering design. Additionally, APL is designed to be interactive in the sense that it is intended to be used by a programmer who is developing, testing and modifying programs at the keyboard. The user is encouraged to try out ideas, and any errors are treated in a friendly and helpful fashion. In this way, APL encourages the programming of the 'what if?' kind of investigative test cases that can help a manager, planner or designer to come to a decision.

The fact that APL can handle arrays as single items contributes to another characteristic of the language, which is that programs written in it tend to be concise. Even for quite complex computations, the programs can be short. This conciseness can be seen both as an advantage and as a drawback. It is usually relatively simple to determine the structure of a short program and, in general, it also takes less time to develop it. The main drawback is that concise programs are hard to understand, and therefore to modify. The power of APL is most easily demonstrated by powerful but concise programs, but such demonstrations can also give the impression that APL is a difficult language. However, I would say that although APL *is* different it is no more difficult to learn than any other language of comparable power.

It has been remarked of other programming languages featured in this book that there is a balance between the conciseness and the readability of the programs written in them. APL, in particular, lends itself to extremely clever tricks with the aid of which a computation can be described extremely briefly. In a program intended for use by no-one except the originator this is admirable, but if the program is to be used by anyone else, and, in particular, if it may need modification, then it is surely more important that it be readable than that it be concise. In any event, APL programs do need to be well documented.

It is characteristic of APL that it relies heavily on its operators, and this has many consequences, a few of which relate to the points discussed above. First, the operators contribute towards making programs short because a particular problem is programmed by employing the operator that is most suitable. Second, APL can be learnt part by part because only the part of it that is actually needed for a particular application needs to be understood. It is possible to learn the language in small pieces because each part is independent of all the others. Most languages do not possess this kind of modularity. Third, to represent its large number of operators, APL has a special character set so that each character can be represented by a single special character. This means that APL programs appear very strange to those unfamiliar with the language. It also means that a special APL keyboard is needed to give these special characters. It is not absolutely essential to have an APL keyboard because there are 'ASCII equivalents' for every APL character, so that APL programs can be entered from a standard keyboard. However, since the notation of APL is so much a part of the language itself, any serious APL user must come to think in terms of its notation, and the interactive use of the language must surely be severely handicapped by the lack of an appropriate keyboard.

The language and some programs

The character set which is used to give the APL notation consists of the letters, numbers and the special characters shown in *Fig. 3.6*: most of the special symbols are used to represent operators. The output from a short dialogue with APL is shown in *Fig. 3.7*; it is intended to illustrate the use of the operators as well as the interactive nature of the language.

When APL is ready to accept information from the keyboard it outputs six spaces. A line is then entered by typing it out and pressing RETURN. APL's response is then given on the next line starting at the left margin. Thus, in *Fig. 3.7* alternate lines show the user's input and APL's response. When an expression involving an operator is entered, APL evaluates the expression and returns its value. The first four entries involve the arithmetic operators, and the asterisk in the fifth entry denotes exponentiation, or 'raising to the

+ x ← [ ] , . /

·· ‾ < ≤ = ≥ > ≠ ∨ ∧ − ÷

? ω ∈ ρ ∼ ↑ ↓ ι ○ * →

a ⌈ ⌊ _ ∇ △ • ' ⎕ ( )

⊂ ⊃ ∩ ∪ ⊥ ⊤ | ; : \

Fig. 3.6. Characters representing APL operators

```
        6+2
8
        6−2
4
        6×2
12
        6÷2
3
        6*2
36
        6⌊2
2
        6⌈2
6
        5×2+4
30
        (5+4+3)÷3
4
        X←10

        X
10
```

Fig. 3.7. Dialogue with APL

power'. The following entry includes the 'minimum' operator, which returns the smaller of its arguments, while the entry after that contains the 'maximum' operator. The eighth entry illustrates that APL always tackles expressions from right to left, so that $5\times2+4$ is evaluated by doing the addition first and then the multiplication. This does not correspond with arithmetic usage in BASIC or FORTRAN, where the correct priority is automatically assigned to arithmetic operators, nor does it correspond to Reverse Polish Notation, which is the other arithmetic system commonly employed among programming languages. The next entry shows that brackets can be used as required in expressions. The left-pointing arrow in the penultimate entry indicates an assignment. After a value has been assigned to a variable, the value can be retrieved simply by entering the name of the variable. APL signals an error if an attempt is made to access the value in a variable before an assignment has been made to it.

The simple and consistent way in which APL deals with lists and vectors is illustrated by the dialogue given in *Fig. 3.8*. A list of numbers is a sequence of numbers each of which is separated by one or more spaces. The first entry shown in *Fig. 3.8* causes 3 to be added to each item in the following list, while the second causes each item to be multiplied by three. In the next entry, the corresponding items of two lists of the same length are added, while in the following entry the maximum of each corresponding pair is found. Assigning a list to a variable is achieved in the same way as assigning a single value.

Fig. 3.8. Dialogue involving lists

Typing the name of the variable then gives the list. The operator in the next entry causes APL to return the number of items in the list assigned to X. The last entry illustrates what is known in APL as 'reduction'. The effect is that the operator preceding the slash is applied to the succeeding list in the same way as if it were placed between all the items of the list. \

APL can handle characters in exactly the same fashion as numbers, and a dialogue illustrating the use of some of the APL operators intended for this purpose is shown in *Fig. 3.9*. The entries show two assignments of character strings to variables and then the use of the operators for concatenation, finding the length of a string and,

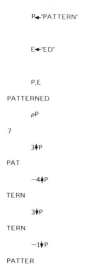

P←'PATTERN'

E←'ED'

P,E
PATTERNED
ρP
7
3↑P
PAT
−4↑P
TERN
3↓P
TERN
−1↓P
PATTER

Fig. 3.9. Dialogue involving character manipulation

lastly, two examples each of the operators for 'taking' and 'dropping'. The up-arrow operator directs that the indicated number of characters should be taken from a string. They are taken from the left or the right end according as the number used is positive or negative. The down-arrow indicates that the characters should be dropped, using the same convention. The facilities illustrated are equivalent to the BASIC functions LEN, LEFT\$ and RIGHT\$.

Fig. 3.10 shows an APL 'one-liner' which is displayed alongside the approximately equivalent BASIC program to illustrate the compactness of the APL program. The programs accept and store a list of numbers, find their average and print it out. The only new symbol in the APL program is the square, which causes APL to accept the list of numbers typed at the keyboard until RETURN is pressed.

```
         10  INPUT N
         20  DIM L(N)
         30  FOR K = 1 TO N
         40  INPUT L (K)
(+/L) ÷ ρL ←↑    50  NEXT K
         60  S = 0
         70  FOR K = 1 TO N
         80  S = S + L (K)
         90  NEXT K
        100  PRINT S/N
        110  END
```

Fig. 3.10. APL one-liner and equivalent BASIC program

Because APL possesses a wide range of operators it has no need of the constructs possessed by such languages as Pascal and BASIC for purposes such as repetition and decision-making. This makes APL an extremely distinctive language. Its distinctiveness often requires a different approach to tackling problems. A change of approach to problem solving may not always be welcomed by those who have to change, but the rewards that follow from it can include improved solution methods and even solutions to previously intractable problems. Although APL permits computations to be described with extreme brevity, so that the resulting programs are hopelessly difficult to understand, Iverson himself has asserted that it is possible to make APL programs at least as readable as those written in other languages by avoiding complex single lines and by providing proper documentation.

Implementations of APL

Not too many implementations of APL are available for the popular microcomputers, but there are several versions commercially available for Z80-based micros. A purpose-designed micro-APL system called MAPLE is also available.

PROLOG

PROLOG is a computer language which originated in a university Artificial Intelligence department and its use for most of its early years was within the confines of similar departments. It was originally developed at The University of Aix-Marseilles in France. Since 1972 implementations of the language have been in use there and also at other places, including The Department of Artificial Intelligence at Edinburgh University and The Department of Computing and Control at Imperial College, London.

PROLOG (PROgramming in LOGic) is a simple, but powerful computer language which was originally developed to help in automatic theorem-proving. The use of formal logic to model human reasoning processes is by no means new but, if computers are to be used in their investigation, then a suitable language helps considerably. PROLOG can be used to good effect in many areas other than automatic theorem-proving. It can be used as a database interrogation language, or for the automation of deductive reasoning, or as a language to represent information for natural language processing.

Currently PROLOG is much more widely available. For example, it has been implemented for a range of DEC computers, and versions are also available for microcomputers. This wider availability, besides broadening the range of users, has also released the language for use in many application areas other than those originally conceived. Many educational projects, including the use of PROLOG as a tool to teach logic to children, are among the new applications.

Programs in PROLOG

A PROLOG program consists of a number of what are called *clauses*. An example of a clause is:

emerald(X)←gem(X), green(X).

This clause can be read in one of two ways. The arrow '←' can be taken to mean 'if', so that the clause reads 'X is an emerald if X is a gem and X is green'. Note that the comma means 'and': the full stop at the end is obligatory. Alternatively, the clause can be read as 'to show that X is an emerald, show that X is a gem and that X is green'. The first way of interpreting the clause treats it as a declaration. It is essentially a declaration of the relationships between the properties of X which, in this case, must be true if X is an emerald. The second interpretation treats the clause as a procedure. It describes the procedure that must be followed, in this example, to demonstrate that X is an emerald. The reader might like to try to give both interpretations to the following clause.

microcomputer(X)←computer(X), small(X).

There are two variants of the clause. If the part to the right of the arrow is omitted, we obtain a statement that is unconditionally true—there are no if's giving the conditions under which it is true. With this type of clause (the 'data clause'), data can be entered. For example, when compiling a database for microcomputers the following clauses might be useful.

microcomputer(pet)←.
microcomputer(apple)←.

They state, respectively, that the PET is a microcomputer, and that the Apple is a microcomputer.

If the part of a clause to the left of the arrow is omitted, the clause becomes an instruction to find an item satisfying the given conditions. The 'query clause'

←microcomputer(X), colourdisplay(X).

can be interpreted as 'find an X which is a microcomputer and which has a colour display'. This type of clause activates a PRO-LOG program, causing it to search for data items satisfying the given conditions. All solutions are given, or if there is no solution an appropriate message is output.

When PROLOG is used as a database system, data clauses are used to enter the data, ordinary clauses are used to enter relationships between data items, and then query clauses are used to interrogate the database. Similarly, in automatic theorem-proving, axioms are entered in the same way as data; deduction rules, giving the valid ways by which deductions may be made from axioms, are entered as ordinary clauses; and then a hypothesis to be tested is entered as a query clause. Any hypothesis which is shown to be true acquires the status of a theorem, and the way in which PROLOG shows it to be true is its proof.

Table 3.1. The three types of clause as written in standard PROLOG, DEC PROLOG and microPROLOG

Ordinary clause

ruby(X)←gem(X), red(X).
ruby(X):- gem(X), red(X).
ruby(X) if gem(X) and red(X).

Data clause

language(pascal)←.
language(pascal).
language pascal.

Query clause

←microcomputer(X), highresolutiongraphics(X).
?-microcomputer(X), highresolutiongraphics(X).
which((X) microcomputer X and highresolutiongraphics X).

Different versions of PROLOG have different ways of representing the three types of clause, mainly because of the different keyboard character sets that are available with various machines. Table 3.1 shows the way each type of clause is written, first as described above, then as in the DEC implementation and thirdly as in microPROLOG. MicroPROLOG was developed at Imperial College, London.

Forming a database using PROLOG

The way in which a database can be established and then interrogated using PROLOG is illustrated in this section. The family tree presented in *Fig. 3.11* provides the data to be held in the database.

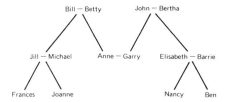

Fig. 3.11. Family tree

The information about this family and its members is to be stored in such a way that queries about family relationships and the relations of members of the family to each other can be answered automatically. The program given in *Fig. 3.12* enters the family tree at lines 100 to 1600 by recording the father and mother of everyone mentioned in the tree. The first data clause

father (garry, john).

can be read as 'the father of Garry is John'. The program also includes at lines 2100 to 2800 various definitions of family relationships that are true in general so that the database can be examined using these relationships. Lines 2100 and 2200 assert that the parent of X is Y either if the mother of X is Y or if the father of X is Y. Line 2300 states that the grandmother of X is Z if the parent of X is Y and the mother of Y is Z. The definition of a sibling is given in line 2500, and it may be read as 'X and Y are siblings if they have the same mother and they are different persons'. The definitions of uncle and aunt require the sex of the person concerned to be specified. For most of the family this information is implicitly recorded already, since mothers are female and fathers are male. Lines 2800

```
00100     father(garry, john).
00200     mother(garry, bertha).
00300     father(elisabeth, john).
00400     mother(elisabeth, bertha).
00500     father(nancy, barrie).
00600     mother(nancy, elisabeth).
00700     father(ben, barrie).
00800     mother(ben, elisabeth).
00900     father(anne, bill).
01000     mother(anne, betty).
01100     father(michael, bill).
01200     mother(michael, betty).
01300     father(frances, michael).
01400     mother(frances, jill).
01500     father(joanne, michael).
01600     mother(joanne, jill).
01700
01800
01900
02000
02100     parent(X, Y):-mother(X, Y).
02200     parent(X, Y):-father(X, Y).
02300     grandmother(X, Z):-parent(X, Y), mother(Y, Z).
02400     grandfather(X, Z):-parent(X, Y), father(Y, Z).
02500     sibling(X, Y):-mother(X, Z), mother(Y, Z), X\==Y.
02600     aunt(X, Z):-parent(X, Y), sibling(Y, Z), female(Z).
02700     uncle(X, Z):-parent(X, Y), sibling(Y, Z), male(Z).
02800     male(M):-father(X, M).
02900     female(F):-mother(X, F).
03000     male(garry).
03100     female(anne).
```

Fig. 3.12. PROLOG program for entering data

and 2900 record this while lines 3000 and 3100 explicitly give the sex
of people in the family tree who are not parents. Actually the definitions of uncle and aunt are not complete, since the husband of an
aunt is an uncle and the wife of an uncle is an aunt, but it is not difficult to add a few more clauses to complete these definitions.

 Fig. 3.13 gives a dialogue that results from interrogating this
database. The first query clause instructs PROLOG to find any X
such that X is a sibling of Nancy. The query clause

?-female(X).

given later requires PROLOG to find all X such that X is female.
Some names appear twice because they are mothers twice, so that
PROLOG finds that they are female in two different ways. The sub-
sequent query

?-grandmother(X, Y).

requires that all the pairs X and Y such that the grandmother of X is
Y be found, and all four pairs are duly found.

72

```
! ?- sibling(nancy, X).

X = ben ;

no
! ?- sibling(garry, X).

X = elisabeth ;

no
! ?- uncle(ben, X).

X = garry ;

no
! ?- aunt(joanne, X).

X = anne ;

no
! ?- grandfather(ben, X).

X = john ;

no
! ?- female(X).

X = bertha ;

X = bertha ;

X = elisabeth ;

X = elisabeth ;

X = betty ;

X = betty ;

X = jill ;

X = jill ;

X = anne ;

no
! ?- grandmother(X, Y).

X = nancy,
Y = bertha ;

X = ben,
Y = bertha ;

X = frances,
Y = betty ;

X = joanne,
Y = betty ;

no
```

Fig. 3.13. Database interrogation using PROLOG

73

Adding the further clauses

descendant (X, Y) :- parent (Y, X).
descendant (X, Z):- parent (Y, X), descendant (Y, Z).

which give a recursive definition of descendant, queries such as those shown in *Fig. 3.14* can be used to trace all the descendants of any individual.

```
! ?- descendant(john, X).

X = garry ;

X = elisabeth ;

X = nancy ;

X = ben ;

no
! ?- descendant(betty, X).

X = anne ;

X = michael ;

X = frances ;

X = joanne ;

no
! ?- descendant(garry, X).

no
```

Fig. 3.14. Interrogation for descendants

How does PROLOG work?

PROLOG stores all ordinary clauses and data clauses. When it is given a query clause such as

?-mother (ben, X).

it searches for a value of X such that mother (ben, X) is true. All possible values for X are tried, so that if there is more than one solution, all of them will be found. Clearly, Ben has only one mother, and she was given in a data clause, so that putting X=elisabeth gives mother (ben, elisabeth), which matches a data clause and so is true, whereas all other values for X fail to produce a match. When given the query clause

?-grandmother (ben, Z).

the process is rather more complex. A value for Z must be found such that parent (ben, Y) and mother (Y, Z) are both true at the

74

same time. So now PROLOG tries all the pairs of values for Y and Z, and reports any values of Z it finds in a successful matching pair of values for Y and Z.

In this way, PROLOG operates by substituting values for the variables in a query clause, and then seeking to match the resulting clause against a data clause, which it has already stored, to determine if there are values for the variables in the query clause that can make it true. Further, ordinary clauses describe the way in which a problem may be solved by solving each of a set of simpler problems.

Besides providing the facilities for establishing and interrogating a database, PROLOG has also been widely used in Artificial Intelligence, and when used for automatic theorem-proving has uncovered unexpected proofs for theorems on more than one occasion.

Implementations of PROLOG

An implementation of PROLOG is available under CP/M, and micro PROLOG, referred to above, is in use at Imperial College, London.

COBOL

COBOL (COmmon Business Oriented Language) is a language for business computing and commercial data processing. The pre-eminence of COBOL in these areas stems from the US Government policy that required the provision of a COBOL compiler with any computer purchased with their funding. As a commercial language, COBOL emphasises the handling of alphanumeric data and files so that tasks such as reading and updating files of records and automatic form filling can be accomplished.

The language is intended to be readable, and supports instructions such as

MOVE X TO Y.

that cause single values or complete structures to be moved. COBOL possesses the usual arithmetic capabilities as well as being able to describe arithmetic operations in a readable way. A formula such as

$x = a + 2b/c$

can be programmed as

COMPUTE X=A+2*B/C

or as

DIVIDE C INTO B GIVING D.
MULTIPLY 2 BY D.
ADD D TO A GIVING X.

In the latter, the programmer must place the instructions in the correct order himself to obtain the desired result. COBOL also provides READ and WRITE instructions for input and output, and conditional instructions such as

IF ORDER IS GREATER THAN 100
MULTIPLY DISCOUNT BY PRICE.

It also provides sophisticated data structures, supporting structures such as the one shown in *Fig. 3.15* from which an item is selected by, for example,

LAST-NAME IN NAME IN EMPLOYEE

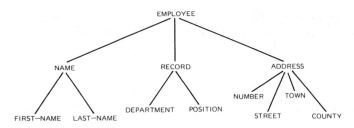

Fig. 3.15. COBOL data structure

COBOL programs have four different divisions, including separate data divisions and procedure divisions. A file called CARDS with records called VALUE each of which contains a single number, PRICE, of up to four digits can be declared in the data division by

FD   CARDS
     DATA RECORD IS VALUE.
01   VALUE.
     01 PRICE PICTURE 9999.

When a file of these records, each containing a single number, has been created, the largest number stored in the file can be found in the procedure division by

     MOVE ZEROS TO A.
READ-IN.
     READ CARDS AT END GO TO LABEL.
     IF PRICE IS GREATER THAN A

76

```
      MOVE PRICE TO A.
      GO TO READ-IN.
  LABEL.
      WRITE A.
```

A file suitable for use in a program to translate English words to the corresponding French words, with records each of which contains an English word and the corresponding French word, can be declared by

```
FD  WORDS
    DATA RECORD IS PAIR.
01  PAIR.
    02  ENGLISH PICTURE IS A(15).
    02  FRENCH PICTURE IS A(15).
```

A translation program that uses this file could have the form

```
START.
      READ WORDS AT END GO TO FINISH.
      IF ENGLISH IS EQUAL TO "CHAIR"
      WRITE FRENCH.
FINISH.
```

Implementations of COBOL

COBOL implementations for micros provide some facilities that are superior to those of mainframe COBOLs such as screen control, so that a 'split' screen can be maintained, and the automatic generation of record descriptions from designs prepared on the screen. CIS COBOL is available under CP/M and Microsoft Standard COBOL is available for the Apple, among others.

FORTH

FORTH was devised by the American astronomer, Charles Moore, as a language for writing programs to control radio telescopes and other astronomical equipment. Although it was originally developed for control applications, it has been adopted by increasing numbers of hobby enthusiasts because it is fast and also because it is an extensible language to which features that it does not already possess can easily be added in such a way that they effectively become part of it. Having this sort of flexibility, FORTH can be readily tailored for any application.

FORTH is a so-called threaded language, which means that the features it provides are maintained as a linked list of items. In this list the name of each item is stored with a machine code routine to provide that facility, and as a result FORTH programs can be executed almost as quickly as machine code programs. Any new feature can simply be added to the linked list, thereby becoming a part of the language and indistinguishable from the original part. When a new feature is defined in terms of other, existing, ones, its name need only be stored together with pointers to the relevant machine code routines to provide the machine code for the new feature.

Using FORTH

Two numbers are added together by the following FORTH program.

5 2 + .

When this program is entered FORTH responds with

7 OK

In running programs FORTH maintains a stack, and when the program above is run, 5 is pushed onto the top of the stack followed by 2. The '+' operator causes the top two items on the stack to be removed, added together and the result to be put on the top of the stack. The operator ' . ' removes the item on the top of the stack and sends it to the display screen. *Fig. 3.16a* represents the state of the

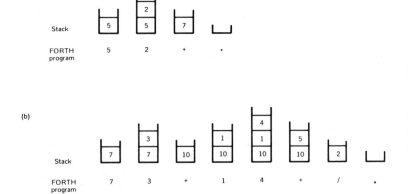

Fig. 3.16. States of the stack during FORTH programs for arithmetic computations

stack during the execution of this program. From FORTH's use of a stack it follows that arithmetic expressions must be written in Reverse Polish form in FORTH programs. The program to evaluate

$(7+3)/(1+4)$

is

7 3 + 1 4 + / .

The states of the stack throughout this computation are shown in *Fig. 3.16b*.

Among the words provided by FORTH in its so-called dictionary it is not surprising to find facilities for manipulating the contents of the stack. They include the words given in Table 3.2.

Table 3.2. FORTH words for stack manipulation

FORTH word	Effect of word
DUP	Makes a copy of the word on the top of the stack, pushing it on top of the original
OVER	Puts a copy of the second item in the stack on the top of the stack
SWAP	Exchanges the top two items on the stack
ROT	Rotates the top three items on the stack by removing the third item and putting it on the top of the stack
DROP	Removes the item on the top of the stack and 'loses' it

The following examples illustrate the use of these words. The states of the stack during the execution of these programs is shown in *Fig. 3.17*.

A number can be squared by

7   DUP * .
49 OK

The value of $(4+6)*4$ can be computed by

4   6 OVER SWAP + * .
40 OK

The operation of ROT is illustrated by

2 4 6 ROT + * .
32   OK

A new FORTH word can be created by, for example:

: CUBE DUP DUP * * ;

This has the general form

  : name definition ;

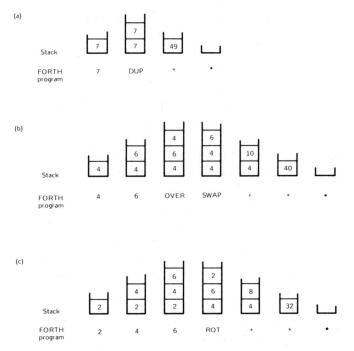

Fig. 3.17. States of the stack during FORTH program using FORTH words

and the colon and semicolon are both FORTH words, denoting the beginning and end of a definition. Once created, a new word can be used in the same way as any other FORTH word, so that the cube of a number could now be computed with

    3   CUBE .
    27   OK

In this way complete programs can consist of a single FORTH word, and the structure of the program consists of the way that other words are combined to give that word. FORTH also provides facilities for repetition and decision-making so that computations involving these can be described directly.

FORTH is an interactive language; programs written in it can be developed quickly and will run more rapidly than comparable programs written in other high-level languages. The flexibility of the language, which permits a vocabulary of words suitable for a particular application to be built up, makes it a language which can be used to advantage in many areas.

Implementations of FORTH

The FORTH language is in the public domain. It has been implemented mainly for micros, and implementations exist for all the major microprocessors including the 8080, Z80 and 6502. The implementations available for popular microcomputers include versions of fig-FORTH for the Sharp MZ80K and the PET, and MMS FORTH for the Tandy TRS80 and Video Genie.

Self-test questions

1. Write program fragments in each of the languages covered in this chapter, except PROLOG, to compute and give the value of the arithmetic expression

$(6+2\times3)/(4-2)$

2. The Lisp function EQUAL is applied to two arguments; it is true if the arguments are the same and false otherwise. Explain the purpose of the function, FUN, defined by

```
(DEFINE (FUN A L)
   (COND ( (NULL    L)         F  )
         ( (EQUAL    (CAR L) A) T)
         ( T              (FUN A (CDR L)))
                                      ))
```

3. Write the APL fragment to cause the word 'INTELLIGENCE' to be stored and processed so that 'TELL' can be printed out.

4. In a game of 'scissors, paper and stone' each of two players makes an independent selection from the three items: a win is obtained on the basis that scissors cut paper, paper wraps stone, or stone blunts scissors. A tie results if the two selections are the same. Write PRO-LOG clauses for describing a game and to give the conditions for deciding if it is a win, tie or loss.

5. Define COBOL files to hold records
   (a) of the type POINT, and
   (b) of the type LINE
as given in question 8(a) of Chapter 2.

6(a) What result is given by this FORTH program?

   4 2 8 DUP ROT + ROT DROP * .

   (b) Create a FORTH word which, when applied to a value of x, will give the value of x^3+3x^2+2x+5.

4
Languages for special applications

The languages covered in Chapters 2 and 3 are all general-purpose languages with which any computation can be described. They can therefore be used for any sort of computation, albeit with a greater or lesser degree of convenience. Programs for any particularly specialised application can be written more easily using a language specifically designed for the purpose. This is particularly true when the application involves the use or control of devices attached to the computer. In this situation signals must be generated by the computer and then communicated to the attached device, so that there must be general agreement between the computer and the peripheral device on several matters including the signal format, precisely where the signals come from and go to, and how the interconnection is to be achieved. It is simpler to write programs for applications of this type if these matters have all been agreed on, and then embedded in a particular language, rather than to use a general-purpose language and to have to take all the constraints into account on every occasion.

In this chapter descriptions are given of three languages, available for microcomputers, designed specifically for graphics, robotics and computer-assisted learning. The graphics language, GINO-F, is for writing programs to generate pictures. Since pictures are produced by drawing lines and curves, special commands not generally possessed by ordinary computing languages must be provided. Sometimes extra commands for these purposes have been added to existing languages, particularly to the versions of BASIC available for various microcomputers. While this is an entirely practical way to provide access to the graphics facilities of a micro, it is not always absolutely satisfactory, in part because the micro manufacturers have all provided the facilities in slightly different ways. A graphics language such as GINO-F not only provides a standard way of adding graphics facilities to a computing language, but also gives all the advantages that follow from having a coherent and logical language for the purpose.

With micros the graphic images are usually generated on the display screen, whether it is an integral screen or the screen of an attached monitor or television set. To this extent, generating the display is a matter that is internal to the computer, but a good graphics language can make it possible to produce the image on a graph plotter, so that a permanent copy of it can be made, quite as easily as on the display screen. If a language provides the capability to generate an image and to direct it to any display device as required, then its advantages over a system that requires separate programs to display the same image on different devices are readily apparent. As good quality graph plotters for use with micros become more readily available from manufacturers such as Watanabe and Hewlett-Packard, this kind of flexibility in the use of graphics becomes more important.

The robotics language, WSFN, is intended for robot control. It provides a compact set of commands for purposes such as instructing a robot to move along a fixed path or to explore its environment, taking particular actions when it encounters an obstacle. What this language provides is, in a sense, a particularly convenient way of generating the signals necessary to control the movements of a robot. Besides causing the computer to send the necessary signals to the robot, the language also takes care of the way in which the computer should handle signals from the robot, typically signals coming from its sensors. In this way, the details of how the computer and the robot communicate are hidden from the programmer, who need only decide what objectives the robot must achieve and how, in general terms, it should achieve them. The detailed means of achieving them are built into the language as far as the fine points of the electronics and the communications signals are concerned. These detailed means of controlling the robot are automatically carried out when the necessary commands are expressed in the programming language.

The third language to be examined is Pilot. It is intended as a language for generating displays and dialogues so that the user of a Pilot program can learn about the subject of the program by, typically, reading frames of information on the subject and then responding to questions about them. The user's responses are examined, and the dialogue proceeds accordingly, as the response reveals how well the information is understood. The computer-assisted learning programs that can be written in Pilot follow, in principle, the form of a programmed text where a page of information is followed by a question and, depending on the answer to the question, the reader is then directed to another page. Computer-assisted learning programmes must justify their existence by being more successful, and by being able to offer more, than a book. That computer-assisted learning *can* offer more than a programmed text is not in question, since the former, by definition, requires a computer which is an extremely flexible device, whereas once a book has been read there are not too many other uses to which it can be put. Whether Pilot is the computer-assisted learning language to release this potential is another matter, and is discussed later in this chapter. The ways in which a computer can improve on a book are, broadly, by accepting wider ranges of answers to the questions (programmed texts tend to offer multiple-choice questions) and by giving a more varied and imaginative range both of rewards for correct answers and of encouragement to proceed after an incorrect response.

The specialist languages examined in this chapter have been chosen because they are all implemented for micros. There are many other areas where common usage may well lead to the introduction of further specialist languages. These areas include, among others, communications, computer-aided design and instrument control. The fact that, for example, there are languages available on mainframe computers especially for computer-aided design, suggests that if sufficient demand develops for this application on micros, then such languages are likely to be implemented for micros. The communications area is also expanding rapidly with increasing interest being shown in microcomputer networks, using micros to access Prestel, and linking micros to mainframe computers via the telephone network to consult databases or to exchange messages. Again, these are all activities of a kind that has interested the conventional computer community for much longer than they have occupied the microcomputer world. Since so much expertise, including language expertise, already exists in this area it may well be borrowed, or adapted, again.

Graphics

The graphics language GINO-F

GINO-F is a general-purpose graphics language. It is not a formal computer language in the sense that all the languages mentioned in previous chapters of this book are, for, whereas languages such as BASIC, Pascal and FORTRAN are completely self-contained, GINO-F consists of a set of subroutines that can be called from a FORTRAN program. Also, in contrast to the general-purpose languages which provide the programmer with all the tools necessary to describe any computation, GINO-F provides routines with the help of which any graphic display can be generated. However, many graphics programs consist of calls to the required GINO-F routines within a minimal FORTRAN framework, so that to this extent GINO-F can be regarded as a graphics language.

Graphics programs are written by combining its routines in much the same way as assembly code programs are written by combining assembly code instructions. Graphic displays can be produced on a number of devices, including high-resolution screens and graph plotters. When a GINO-F program is run, it generates the commands to cause the display device that is being used to exhibit the required image. The analagous situation with an assembly code program is that when it is run, it causes the processor that is being used to exhibit the required behaviour when it obeys the successive assembly code instructions.

A graphics package called GINO preceded GINO-F: it was developed at Cambridge University and was written in Assembler. Its name is derived from the words Graphical INput and Output, which describe the function of the package. The C.A.D. Centre at Cambridge subsequently developed GINO-F, which is a more systematically designed package that provides for all the commonly used graphical activities rather than just for input and output. It is written in FORTRAN (hence the F in its name), and as well as being a graphics language it permits graphical displays to be generated by existing programs merely by incorporating the appropriate GINO-F elements.

The package was originally intended for use on mainframe computers, but it has now been released in a microcomputer version for the Research Machines 380Z. As the resolution of microcomputer displays improves, and also as good quality graph plotters become more readily available for micros, the need for a coherent graphics language to be available for any micro is likely to be increasingly felt. The graphics facilities possessed by most micros are usually accessed by extra commands that have been added to the BASIC of the micro. This results in micros such as the Apple, the Acorn Atom, the BBC Microcomputer, the Atari 800 and the Hewlett-Packard HP85 all possessing different graphics commands. However, it is interesting to observe that many of the commands added to these BASICs are quite heavily influenced by the facilities possessed by GINO-F and other similar graphics languages.

The facilities of GINO-F

GINO-F is available for a wide range of large computers, so that it provides for them the portability of graphics programs that is so completely lacking in microcomputer graphics. The language also permits graphics programs to be written that are essentially independent of the display device that is being used: merely by nominating the display device at the beginning of the graphics part of the program, the output can appear on any one of a high-resolution monochrome display screen, a colour screen or a graph plotter. Elements that do not apply to the particular display device that is being used, such as colour commands to a monochrome display device, will simply be ignored.

The facilities provided by GINO-F can be classified into the following six groups:

1. *Administrative*. This group includes the facilities for naming the output device, so that all the commands that are generated by the graphics program when it is run will be for the display device that is to exhibit the picture. It also includes facilities for establishing the scale of the picture that is to be drawn, and for ending the graphics part of a program.

2. *Two-dimensional drawing*. The facilities for drawing lines and curves, and for moving the drawing head to any location without drawing a line are all in this group. These commands are sufficient to produce any picture, graph or figure.

3. *Three-dimensional drawing*. The facilities for three-dimensional drawing permit any three-dimensional object to be described. The object can be displayed on a (two-dimensional) display surface when the position from which it is observed and the perspective transformation to be used have both been established.

4. *Transformations*. Besides the projective transformations for displaying three-dimensional objects, this group includes the rotational, scaling and shifting transformations for both two- and three-dimensional objects. When a transformation is invoked in a program, it applies to all the drawing commands that follow it. Thus, if the transformation to rotate by 45 degrees is invoked, then everything that is drawn subsequently is rotated through 45 degrees. The transformations are typically used to reveal different views of an object in applications such as computer-aided design or to facilitate animation.

5. *Character output*. With these facilities, characters can be included in a graphic display, for example to label a graph. The size, shape and orientation of the characters can be established independently from the rest of the graph.

6. *Interaction*. These facilities permit interaction with a graphics program, for example by means of a light pen.

Some simple programs

To illustrate the way in which graphics programs are written using GINO-F and to demonstrate its capabilities, some simple graphics programs are presented. When drawing a picture, whether with the aid of a computer or not, one's first concerns must include the positioning of the picture on the display surface and its scaling. Gauging either of these incorrectly can obviously have dire consequences, such as the picture not fitting onto the surface or being so small that it cannot be seen properly.

The size of the display area will vary from device to device, but any point in the area can be located by giving its distance from the left-hand edge of the area (referred to in geometrical terms as its x-coordinate) and its distance from the bottom edge (its y-coordinate). *Fig. 4.1* illustrates the location of the point with an x-coordinate of

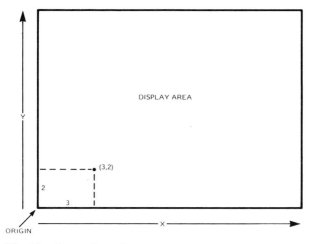

Fig. 4.1. Axes and coordinates

3 and a y-coordinate of 2, usually called the point with coordinates (3,2). The point with coordinates (0,0), which in this case is the bottom left-hand corner of the drawing area, is referred to as the origin. At the start of every GINO-F program the origin is situated at the bottom left-hand corner of the display area, as one would expect, and the plotting units are millimetres. However, the language provides facilities for relocating the origin and for resetting the plotting units if there are more convenient alternatives. In this way, GINO-F provides the tools for handling positioning and scaling; it not only provides a default situation, but also gives the means to alter it to be more convenient.

Now let us examine the problem of writing a program to draw a square with sides of length two centimetres with its bottom left-hand corner situated three centimetres above the bottom left-hand corner of the display area and three centimetres to its right on a Hewlett-Packard graph plotter. The program should start by nominating the graph plotter as the display device. The natural origin is probably satisfactory but, as the problem is specified in centimetres, it is convenient to alter the plotting units to centimetres. The square can be drawn by moving the pen to one of its corners and then drawing a line from one corner to the next until the four sides of the square are all drawn. The graphics part of the program can then be ended. As a result of this, the following simple program to draw a square is obtained.

```
CALL HP7220
CALL UNITS(10.0)
CALL MOVTO2(3.0,3.0)
CALL LINTO2(3.0,5.0)
CALL LINTO2(5.0,5.0)
CALL LINTO2(5.0,3.0)
CALL LINTO2(3.0,3.0)
CALL DEVEND
STOP
END
```

Note that the graphics part of the program consists of a sequence of calls to GINO-F subroutines. The names of the subroutines usually more or less explain their functions. The first call nominates the HP7220 graph plotter as the output device (some of the diagrams in this chapter were drawn using this Hewlett-Packard plotter). The second call alters the plotting units to 10 times their default value, that is, to 10 millimetres or one centimetre. The next call moves the pen, but with the pen up so that it does not draw a line, to the point with coordinates (3,3). The next four calls each cause lines to be drawn from the current position of the pen to the point whose coordinates are given in the command. The call to DEVEND terminates the graphics part of the program, while the last two lines are required to terminate a FORTRAN program.

The whole program for drawing a square is a FORTRAN program. The graphics part of the program is a series of subroutines called from the FORTRAN program, and this is possible because the GINO-F subroutines are all written in FORTRAN themselves. The same drawing can be produced on any other device simply by naming that device at the beginning of the graphics part of the program. Although the concept of moving a pen with the pen up or down does not apply literally to producing images on a high-resolution display screen, one can invoke the equivalent idea of controlling a drawing head that can either leave a trace, or not, as it moves. A selection of GINO-F routines and their effects is listed in Table 4.1.

Table 4.1. GINO-F subroutines

Name	Purpose
CHAANG (ANGLE)	Sets orientation of characters to ANGLE
CHAHOL ('STRING*.')	Outputs the string STRING
CHASIZ (CHAWID,	
CHAHIG)	Sets character size
CURTO2	
(X,Y,NPTS,IB,IF)	Draws a smooth curve through a set of points
DEVEND	Terminates graphical output
HP7220	Nominates HP7220 graph plotter as output device
LINTO2 (X,Y)	Draws a straight line to (X,Y)
LINTO3 (X,Y,Z)	Draws a straight line in three dimensions
MOVTO2 (X,Y)	Positions pen/beam at (X,Y)
MOVTO3 (X,Y,Z)	Positions pen/beam in three dimensions
ROTAT2(ANGLE)	Gives rotation about the origin by ANGLE
SCALE (S)	Gives scaling transformation
SHIFT2 (X,Y)	Gives shift transformation
TRANSF (I)	Transformation control
UNITS (XMILS)	Specifies drawing units
VIEW	Generates view transformation
VPOINT	
(X,Y,Z,DX,DY,DZ)	Sets up a perspective view
VPOSIT (X,Y)	Gives the position for the view image

The pattern displayed in *Fig. 4.2* is produced by joining each of 12 points that are equally spaced round the circumference of a circle to each of the others. The pattern was generated by the following program which joins the points in an order that avoids drawing every line in the pattern twice. For this picture it is useful to have the origin at the centre of the circle, but the origin itself needs to be in the centre of the drawing surface to display the entire pattern. The call to SHIFT2 invokes the transformation which conveniently shifts the pattern into the centre of the plotting area. The program is:

```
      DIMENSION X(12), Y(12)
      ANGLE=0.0
      AINC=6.2831853/12.0
      DO 10 I=1,12
      ANGLE=ANGLE+AINC
      X(I)=8.0*COS(ANGLE)
      Y(I)=8.0*SIN(ANGLE)
   10 CONTINUE
```

```
      CALL HP7220
      CALL UNITS(10.0)
      CALL SHIFT2(12.0,12.0)
      DO 20 I=1,11
      IP1=I+1
      DO 30 J=IP1,12
      CALL MOVTO2(X(I), Y(I))
      CALL LINTO2( X(J), Y(J) )
  30  CONTINUE
  20  CONTINUE
      CALL DEVEND
      STOP
      END
```

This program illustrates clearly the way in which the GINO-F elements can be embedded in a FORTRAN program. The locations of the 12 points around the circle are computed, and the x and y coor-

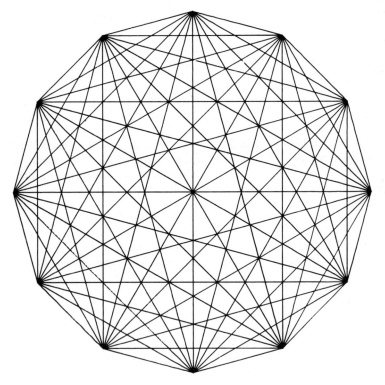

Fig. 4.2. Pattern generated with GINO-F

90

dinates of the points are stored respectively in the arrays X and Y. The points are then joined as required to produce the pattern, and the shift transformation has ensured that the entire pattern is sensibly placed on the drawing surface.

The simple graph shown in *Fig. 4.3* was produced by the next program.

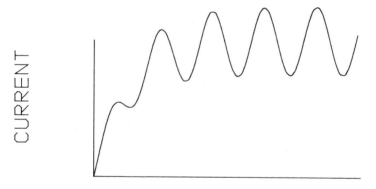

Fig. 4.3. Graph drawn with GINO-F

```
      DIMENSION X(80), Y(80)
      DO 10 I=1, 80
      X(I)=0.1*(I-1)
      Y(I)=4.0*(1.0-EXP(-X(I)))*(1.0+0.25*SIN(4.0*X(I)))
   10 CONTINUE
      CALL HP7220
      CALL UNITS(15.0)
      CALL SHIFT2(4.0,4.0)
      CALL MOVTO2(0.0,4.0)
      CALL LINTO2(0.0,0.0)
      CALL LINTO2(8.0,0.0)
      CALL CURTO2(X,Y,80,0,0)
```

```
CALL CHASIZ(0.4,0.4)
CALL MOVTO2(3.0, −2.0)
CALL CHAHOL('TIME*.')
CALL MOVTO2(1.5,7.0)
CALL CHAHOL('CIRCUIT RESPONSE*.')
CALL MOVTO2(−2.0,1.0)
CALL CHAANG(90.0)
CALL CHAHOL('CURRENT*.')
CALL DEVEND
STOP
END
```

The curve resulted from the call to CURTO2(X,Y,80,0,0): this causes a smooth curve to be drawn through the 80 points with their x and y coordinates respectively stored in the arrays X and Y. The calls following CURTO in the program all deal with the characters used to label the graph. CHASIZ gives the size of the characters by fixing their width and height. Each line of characters is positioned using MOVTO2, and CHAANG can be used to change the angle at which the characters are printed if this is necessary. Finally, the text to be written is included in quotes in a call to CHAHOL, and it must be terminated by an asterisk and a full stop.

Any shape can be drawn by joining together a number of points, so that if the x and y coordinates of these points are stored in arrays X and Y respectively, then a shape can be drawn by a routine such as the following:

```
      SUBROUTINE SHUTTLE
      DIMENSION X(100), Y(100)
      CALL MOVTO2( X(1), Y(1) )
      DO 10 I=2,100
      CALL LINTO2( X(I), Y(I) )
   10 CONTINUE
      RETURN
      END
```

The locations of the points which, when joined, give a particular shape can be measured manually or they can be selected using a digitiser. The use of a digitiser is extremely simple, particularly when compared to the laborious manual method, and digitising tablets are now available for micros, notably for the Apple and HP85. Once a shape is stored it can be drawn again in many ways with the use of the transformations. This is illustrated by the next program fragment, which generated *Fig. 4.4.*

92

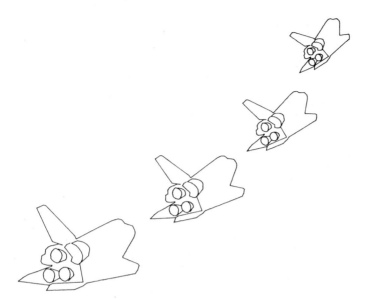

Fig. 4.4. Transforming the Shuttle

```
      DO 50 K=1,4
      CALL SHUTTLE
      CALL SHIFT2(7.0,1.5)
      CALL ROTAT2(10.0)
      CALL SCALE(0.8)
   50 CONTINUE
```

The shuttle is plotted at its correct size once, but it is scaled down, rotated and shifted prior to each of the succeeding plots. Note that the effect of the transformations is cumulative.

Drawing three-dimensional objects

The realistic display of three-dimensional objects on a two-dimensional surface is made quite easy in GINO-F. A three-dimensional object is described by giving the instructions for 'drawing' it in three dimensions. That is, by locating points in space and then saying how they have to be joined in order to describe the object. Before the object is displayed on a screen or plotted, the position from which it is to be viewed and the direction of viewing must

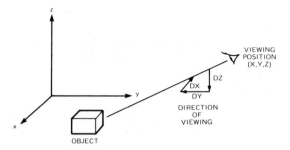

Fig. 4.5. Viewing a three-dimensional object

be given in the way illustrated in *Fig. 4.5* using the routine **VPOINT**. Then calling the transformation routine **VIEW** automatically causes the appropriate perspective view of the object to be generated when the three-dimensional drawing commands are executed. The following program produced the drawings shown in *Fig. 4.6*.

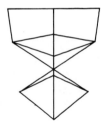

Fig. 4.6. Different views of a goblet

```
      DIMENSION X(4),Y(4),Z(4),U(4),V(4)
      CALL HP7220
      CALL UNITS(12.0)
      DATA X/5.0,0.0,5.0,3.0/
      DATA Y/4.0,5.0,0.0,2.0/
      DATA Z/3.0,3.0,3.0,3.0/
      DATA U/5.0,15.0,5.0,15.0/
      DATA V/5.0,5.0,12.0,12.0/
      DO 10 I=1,4
      D=SQRT( X(I)*X(I)+Y(I)*Y(I)+Z(I)*Z(I) )
      CALL VPOINT(X(I),Y(I),Z(I),-X(I),-Y(I),-Z(I),D)
      CALL VPOSIT(U(I),V(I) )
      CALL VIEW
      CALL MOVTO3(-1.0,-1.0,  1.0)
      CALL LINTO3(  1.0,-1.0,  1.0)
      CALL LINTO3(  1.0,-1.0,-1.0)
      CALL LINTO3(-1.0,-1.0,-1.0)
      CALL LINTO3(-1.0,-1.0,  1.0)
      CALL LINTO3(  1.0,  1.0,-1.0)
      CALL LINTO3(-1.0,  1.0,-1.0)
      CALL LINTO3(-1.0,  1.0,  1.0)
      CALL LINTO3(  1.0,  1.0,  1.0)
      CALL LINTO3(  1.0,  1.0,-1.0)
      CALL LINTO3(  1.0,  2.0,-1.0)
      CALL LINTO3(-1.0,  2.0,-1.0)
      CALL LINTO3(-1.0,  2.0,  1.0)
      CALL LINTO3(  1.0,  2.0,  1.0)
      CALL LINTO3(  1.0,  2.0,-1.0)
      CALL MOVTO3(-1.0,  2.0,-1.0)
      CALL LINTO3(-1.0,  1.0,-1.0)
      CALL LINTO3(  1.0,-1.0,  1.0)
      CALL MOVTO3(  1.0,-1.0,-1.0)
      CALL LINTO3(-1.0,  1.0,  1.0)
      CALL LINTO3(-1.0,  2.0,  1.0)
      CALL MOVTO3(  1.0,  2.0,  1.0)
      CALL LINTO3(  1.0,  1.0,  1.0)
      CALL LINTO3(-1.0,-1.0,-1.0)
      CALL TRANSF(2)
10    CONTINUE
      CALL DEVEND
      STOP
      END
```

The description of the object is embodied in the 24 three-dimensional drawing calls to MOVTO3 and LINTO3. Changing the values in the call to VPOINT allows different views of the object to be obtained. The call to TRANSF(2) is used merely to prevent the perspective transformations produced by VIEW from having a cumulative effect. VPOSIT is used to position the four views on the drawing surface. Interestingly, the process carried out by GINO-F in reducing the description of a three-dimensional object is, in principle, the opposite to what the human brain does in reconstructing a three-dimensional view of the world from the essentially two-dimensional representation that it obtains from the retina of the eye.

The graphics facilities of microcomputer BASICs

GINO-F is available for the Research Machines 380Z, which supports FORTRAN, so that it can run the graphics package in essentially the same form as a mainframe machine. Consequently, at least one micro supports a powerful and coherent graphics language. The high-resolution displays possessed by many micros can exhibit complex and detailed images, and they deserve a language that makes it easy to produce such images. They can, with their existing facilities, produce impressively detailed images: the manual provided with the Acorn Atom includes a program for generating perspective views of a convoluted surface, and the results it produces are quite remarkable. However, it is not at all easy to understand how the program works since all the effects are obtained from first principles, including the perspective transformation. A programmer wanting to understand the techniques of computer graphics will have no objections to the amount of study that may be necessary to understand the program, but it may prove arduous, or even too difficult, for the less expert user wanting only to show, and perhaps slightly modify, the display for a particular purpose.

The graphics commands available on most of the popular micros are provided as extensions of their BASICs. The widely differing nature of the graphics commands that have been provided for various micros can be illustrated quite simply by giving the programs that are broadly equivalent to the GINO-F program for plotting a square that was given earlier. The program for the Apple is:

```
10   HGR:HCOLOR=3
20   HPLOT 30, 30
30   HPLOT TO 30, 50
40   HPLOT TO 50, 50
50   HPLOT TO 50, 30
```

```
60    HPLOT TO 30, 30
```

For the Acorn Atom, the program is

```
10    CLEAR 4
20    MOVE 30, 30
30    DRAW 30, 50
40    DRAW 50, 50
50    DRAW 50, 30
60    DRAW 30, 30
70    END
```

Clearly these two BASICs possess broadly equivalent commands, but a good deal of translation is necessary to convert a graphics program from one version to the other. The drawing commands HPLOT TO 50, 50 and DRAW 50, 50 both cause a line to be drawn from the current position to the dot in column 50 and row 50 of the screen. Consequently, graphic commands must be expressed in terms of screen positions, which is much less convenient than dealing with the actual values to be plotted, as is made possible by GINO-F. A further consequence of dealing with screen positions is that neither of the programs given above actually generates a square! They produce rectangles whose size and shape depend on the shape of the display area and its resolution. Yet another complication with these two programs is that the Atom locates the display origin at the bottom left, as one might expect, whereas the Apple locates it at the top left.

To summarise this, two apparently equivalent programs for plotting a square give rectangles that have different sizes and shapes, and that also occupy different positions on the screen. This confusion is in stark contrast to the control that is presented to the programmer by GINO-F.

The graphics facilities possessed by the Hewlett-Packard HP85 are a definite improvement on those of the Apple, Atom and other similar machines, and it must be said that the HP85 is a Rolls-Royce among micros. The commands in this machine's BASIC include:

SCALE XMIN, XMAX, YMIN, YMAX

which permits the user to set the scale in both x and y directions by giving the actual values that should correspond to the extremities of the plotting area. Plotting can then be carried out using the actual values to be plotted, and the system automatically positions them correctly on the display surface. From the point of view of plotting a square, the command

SHOW XMIN, XMAX, YMIN, YMAX

is even more useful, as it not only offers essentially the same facilities as SCALE, but also provides units of equal length in both directions.

The problems of a language designer trying to decide which graphics commands to add to the BASIC of a particular micro could be resolved by turning to GINO. Although GINO-F is written in FORTRAN, there is no reason why a similar version could not be written in BASIC: such a version would be ideal for micros, providing a general purpose graphics extension that could be added to any BASIC as required. It would give easy access to the high-resolution graphics as well as providing portable graphics programs.

Robotics

One of the most directly appealing applications of a micro to many people is to control a physical object, such as a robot or a Turtle, so that some actual movement can be seen to result from the activity of the micro. The control of a robot is achieved by connecting it to one of the computer's sockets, in the same way as a printer or a disk unit is attached, and then control is achieved by sending signals to it from the computer. A socket such as the 'user port' of the PET is ideal for this purpose because it permits signals to be sent to the robot and to be received from it. A two-way communication channel permits the computer not only to control the robot but also to provide it with a degree of 'intelligence' by running a program which the robot can invoke so as to know how to behave in certain circumstances. For example, if a robot is systematically exploring its environment, it can return a signal to the computer when it touches anything, and this signal can then trigger the computer to send the appropriate commands so that the robot can deal with the situation.

LOGO is a language that is used a good deal in this area, particularly for controlling a Turtle. However, this language is quite similar to Lisp, so rather than describing it, we introduce WSFN which is a language that was devised especially for controlling robots.

The robot control language WSFN

WSFN is intended to be a language in which commands to a microprocessor-controlled robot can be expressed, and then issued using a keyboard as the input device. The language was devised by Lichen Wang and first published in 1977. It possesses only a small number of commands, and all the instructions issued to a robot must be composed from this small repertoire, which includes commands such as 'move forward one step' and 'turn to the right'. However, the language permits these commands to be combined in quite complex ways, so that sophisticated programs can be written despite the smallness of the language. A version of the language is available for controlling a simple robot such as a Turtle. Other versions are written to control a cursor on a screen which can leave a trace to mark its path: such a version can be used either as a robot simulation or as a facility for drawing patterns.

As a robot command language, WSFN provides the robot it controls with a memory and generates the signals that are necessary for the robot to obey the commands issued to it. The memory consists of an accumulator and a facility for storing macros. The accumulator is an eight-bit register: its 256 possible contents are treated as the integers from 0 to 255. A macro is a sequence of commands that is given an associated name. When a macro is defined, it causes the sequence of commands to be stored together with the name. Subsequently, the macro name can be given as a command, and when this is done the name is replaced by the sequence of commands associated with it, and this sequence is then executed. In this way, a macro is a means of extending the language.

The commands to the accumulator are '+' to increment it and '−' to decrement it. Repetition is achieved by preceding the command to be repeated by the number giving the repetitions required. Thus, 27+ means increment the accumulator 27 times. Preceding a command by 'A' indicates that it should be repeated as many times as the number in the accumulator. To illustrate this, A+ causes the number in the accumulator to be doubled, while A− causes the accumulator to be set to zero.

Since setting the accumulator to zero can be a useful facility, it may be worth defining a macro to do it. This is done by giving the commands that achieve it a single letter name that does not clash with the name of any other command, Z say, and then defining the macro by

Z=A−

This stores the macro definition A− in association with the macro name Z, and subsequently, when the command Z is issued, the commands in the macro body are obeyed, setting the accumulator to zero.

In WSFN, brackets can be used to group commands, and blanks are significant, being interpreted as 'no operation' commands, that is, as commands to do nothing.

The fundamental commands for robot movement are 'F' to cause the robot to move forward by one unit and 'R' to cause it to turn 45°

to its right (that is, clockwise as seen from above). These two commands are sufficient to move a robot to any position in its field of activity with a resolution of one unit, and if this unit is comparable in size to the length and width of the robot, then this should be adequate for most purposes. Thus, a robot can be commanded to trace a square of side 4 units as shown in *Fig. 4.7* by the compound command

RRFFFFRRFFFFRRFFFFRRFFFF

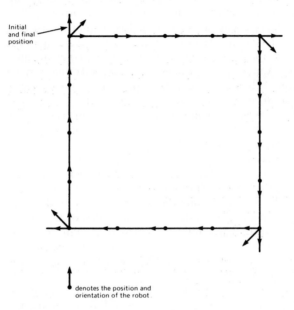

Fig. 4.7. Sequence of positions as the robot moves on a square path

However, using the repetition facility, this could be expressed as

2R4F2R4F2R4F2R4F

and, using brackets, even more compactly as

4(2R4F)

The robot would trace a square path of side 8 units in an anticlockwise direction in response to

4(6R8F)

Additionally, there are two conditional commands denoted by 'T' and 'S'. The conditional command starting with 'T' consists of 'T'

100

followed by two commands and its meaning is 'if the contents of the accumulator are not zero then execute the first command else execute the second command'. This gives the robot the capability to take different actions depending on the contents of the accumulator. The second command gives the ability to take one of two actions depending on whether the robot's sensor is activated. So a command consisting of 'S' followed by a pair of commands means that if the sensor indicates that the robot has touched an obstacle then the first command should be executed otherwise the second should be followed.

All the commands provided by WSFN specifically for robot control have now been described. WSFN envisages a robot which can move and turn, has a rather small memory and a sensor which is activated when an obstacle is touched, and which responds to a small set of commands. The commands are summarised in Table 4.2: with this small repertoire, programs can be written for surprisingly sophisticated tasks.

Table 4.2. The WSFN commands for robot control

Command	Meaning
+	Increment the number in the accumulator
−	Decrement the number in the accumulator
F	Move forward one unit
R	Rotate 45° to the right
( )	Used to group commands
nx	Repeat x n times
Ax	Repeat x by the number in the accumulator
Txy	If the accumulator contents are not zero then execute x else execute y
Sxy	If the sensor is activated then execute x else execute y
	N.B. In this Table, x and y represent commands, and n represents an integer value

There are a few more single character commands which can be added to WSFN when a screen simulation is being controlled rather than a real robot. They are listed in Table 4.3. The remaining examples of WSFN programs are oriented to a screen simulation, simply because the robot can be made to mark its path on the screen so that

Table 4.3. Extra WSFN commands for screen simulations

Command	Meaning
H	Send the robot 'home' to the centre of the screen
N	Make the robot face 'north', or up the screen
C	Clear the screen
V	Make the robot leave a visible trace
I	Make the robot's trace invisible

its route is visible. This makes it far easier to try to understand what is happening than trying to remember the route or to visualise it from a verbal description.

Some example programs

It is always possible to describe to a robot the way in which it should follow a particular path by providing the directions in complete detail. However, it has already been demonstrated that WSFN programs for fairly complex tasks can be made quite compact, and the examples in this section are intended to illustrate this facet of the language further. Since the examples are conceived in terms of a screen simulation, it is useful to define the initialisation macro

D=CHNWA−

which causes the screen to be cleared, places the robot in the centre of the screen facing up it and in a state so that it leaves a white trace when it moves, besides clearing the accumulator. The shape shown in *Fig 4.8a* is traced when the macro

E=10F2R2F2R7F2R2F

is executed. The shape can be incorporated into a larger pattern of the kind shown in *Fig. 4.8b*, which is produced by

D4(HNARE2+)

This program causes the shape to be drawn four times: prior to each one the robot is sent to the centre of the screen and made to face

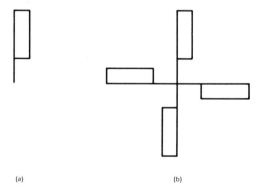

(a)   (b)

Fig. 4.8.   (a) Shape described by macro E (b) Cross pattern from program incorporating E

102

north before turning right as many times as the number in the accumulator. Since the accumulator is incremented twice after the shape is drawn, successive shapes are positioned at 90° to each other. Note that whatever shape is described by E, the program will produce four copies of it in a 'cross' pattern.

A robot faced by an unknown labyrinth that contains only right-angle turns, such as the one illustrated in *Fig. 4.9,* can find its way

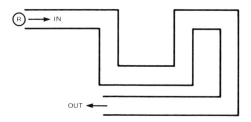

Fig. 4.9. Labyrinth

through it under the command of a program incorporating the conditional instruction which tests the sensor. An algorithm for proceeding through the labyrinth is:

Repeatedly
  if you can, go ahead
    else
      (if you can, turn right and go ahead
        else
          turn left and go ahead)

This can be expressed in WSFN as repeated executions of

S(2RS(4RF)F)F

A similar program can be written to enable a robot to find its way through a maze. A maze is more complex than a labyrinth, since it can contain T-junctions, cross-roads and dead-ends as well as left and right turns. However, a program for exploring a maze need be only slightly more complex than that for a labyrinth.

WSFN supports recursion by allowing a macro to call itself. The way in which recursion is supported is illustrated by the following program for drawing a square spiral, or 'spirolateral'. The spirolateral paths generated by the program are illustrated in *Fig. 4.10:* they can be generated by commanding the robot to advance by a certain number of steps, 10 say, then turn 90° to the right and do the

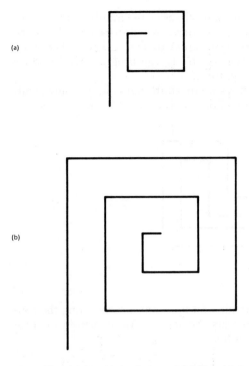

(a)

(b)

Fig. 4.10. (a) Six-sided spirolateral (b) Ten-sided spirolateral

same thing again, but taking one step less, and continuing to do this until the number of steps is reduced to zero. The macro is

M=T(AF2R−M)ƀ

where ƀ denotes a blank or space. The macro will cause the robot to execute the bracketed command if the accumulator contents are not zero, and to do nothing when the accumulator contains zero. The program

D10+M

initialises the robot, sets the accumulator to 10, and produces the spirolateral shown in *Fig. 4.10b*.

When the macro is executed, it causes the accumulator contents to be examined, finds that they are 10, and so are not zero, which causes the bracketed part of the macro to be executed. The robot takes 10 steps forward and turns 90° to the right before the accumulator is decremented and the macro invokes itself. For the second macro call the accumulator contents are 9. Since the accumulator

104

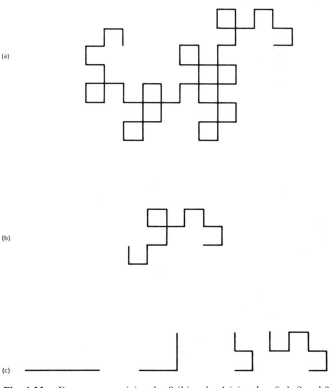

(a)

(b)

(c)

Fig. 4.11. Dragon curves (a) order 8 (b) order 4 (c) orders 0, 1, 2 and 3

contents are decremented just prior to the macro calling itself each time, eventually the contents of the accumulator become zero and the recursion is halted by causing the conditional command which comprises the macro to select the option to do nothing. The number in the accumulator when M is first called determines both the length of the longest side and the number of sides of the spirolateral.

A more complex example of recursion is given by the following macros and program which produced the 'Dragon curve' shown in *Fig. 4.11a.*

L =T(−L6RJ+)G
J =T(−L2RJ+)G
G=4F
D8+L

Fig. 4.11b was produced with the same macros and the program

D4+L

The recursion is more complicated than in the previous example because J invokes L, and L invokes J. A 'Dragon curve' of any order can be generated by setting the accumulator to the required value prior to invoking the macro L. Dragon curves can be made by folding a strip of paper. Folding the strip in half, and then folding it in half again, in the same direction, so that it is a quarter of its original length and so on, will give all the 'Dragon curves' if after each fold the paper is unfolded and arranged so that it has a right angle at each crease. *Fig. 4.11c* shows the first four such curves.

WSFN and micros

Wang published WSFN in *Dr Dobbs' Journal*, numbers 18 and 20, in a pair of articles entitled 'An interactive programming language for control of robots'. The articles include a listing of an implementation of the language written in 8080 assembly code: routines are given for controlling a Turtle and for controlling a cursor in a screen simulation. A version of WSFN written in BASIC was available for the PET (from PetSoft), but it has unfortunately been withdrawn.

WSFN is a small language for an interesting application which includes all the features necessary to construct the essential program 'shapes'. In its own way, it shows the small core that is essential in any programming language. The programs written in WSFN can be concise but can also, as a result, be hard to read and understand. These factors must be balanced against each other in any language, although languages do exist in which it is hard to write programs that are either concise or readable!

Computer-assisted learning (CAL)

For many years attempts have been made to develop machines that could assist in the learning process. A whole generation of so-called 'teaching machines' was almost totally unsuccessful, largely because they were dull and boring to use. I would venture the opinion that a teaching machine of any kind is unlikely ever to improve on the effectiveness of a good teacher because it seems unlikely to me that it can give the variety of explanations and demonstrations that a teacher can, just as it is unlikely that it can present material in a way that is as well adapted to the needs of the learner. However, if any machine can do it, or come near to doing it, that machine is surely the computer. A computer can overcome the problem of boredom because it is not a special-purpose machine and it can offer other facilities to the learner to ward off boredom, to reward a good learning performance or to encourage the less successful.

When computers are found more and more commonly in the home, it would seem a great waste if their potential as educational aids were not fully tapped. The key to using a computer as a learning aid is, of course, to have a fund of good programs for that purpose, and a major necessity if it is to be fairly easy to write CAL programs is to have a good language for writing them. Pilot is a language specifically for writing CAL programs that is widely available on micros. In the following sections the language and the way in which it is used are described, and some discussion of its success as a language is presented.

Pilot

Pilot is a language for writing programs which, when they are run, can help the user to learn a particular topic or subject. The original version of the language was designed at the San Francisco Medical Centre in 1973 and is now known as Core Pilot. In its early years it was used in a fairly pure, standard form for producing interactive dialogues intended for learning purposes. Subsequently, the language has been extended by Professor G. Gerhold and L. Kheriaty to give what is known as Common Pilot. The extended version of the language is more powerful and flexible than the original, and probably deserves to be known as an 'author language' for CAL.

Core Pilot

The Core Pilot version of the language has six types of instruction. In a program, each instruction begins with a key letter or letters which signal the instruction's type; the letter or letters are followed by a colon which simply serves to separate them from the rest of the instruction, which is always written after the colon. The types of instruction, their key letters, and the effects produced when the instructions are executed are tabulated in Table 4.4.

Thus, Core Pilot has instructions for input and output, conditional instructions, a jump instruction with which a loop can be constructed to permit repetition, but its only instruction to permit any processing is its instruction for matching. The lack of powerful instructions for processing limits the language to producing simple dialogues.

To illustrate how these instructions are used in a simple program,

Table 4.4. The instruction types of Core Pilot

Instruction type	Instruction format	Effect of instruction
Output	T: text	Print the text following the colon
Input	A:	Accept a string of characters from the keyboard
Match	M: pattern	Compare the pattern following the colon to the most recently accepted input string; if they match set a special indicator (known as the 'match flag') to Y otherwise set it to N
Jump	J: 0	Jump to the preceding input instruction
Stop	S:	Halt program execution
Conditional	Y	This can precede the initial letter of any instruction; the instruction is then executed only if the match flag is Y
	N	This can precede the initial letter of any instruction; the instruction is then executed only if the match flag is N

the following program causes a question to be printed, accepts an answer which it matches against the correct answer before printing an appropriate comment on the answer.

```
T:   WHAT IS THE SUM OF 2, 4 AND 6?
A:
M:   12
YT:  GOOD. TWELVE IS CORRECT
NT:  NO. THE ANSWER IS 12.
S:
```

A second program using the jump instruction illustrates how more than one opportunity to provide the correct answer can be given. Unless the correct answer is given the jump instruction causes the input instruction to be executed again, thus providing the user with a further opportunity to answer.

```
T:   WHAT IS THE LARGEST COUNTRY IN AFRICA?
A:
M:   SUDAN
YT:  YES, THAT IS CORRECT.
YS:
NT:  NO. TRY AGAIN.
J:   0
```

A typical dialogue produced by running this program is:

```
WHAT IS THE LARGEST COUNTRY IN AFRICA?
?  NIGERIA
NO. TRY AGAIN.
```

? SOUTH AFRICA
NO. TRY AGAIN.
? SUDAN
YES, THAT IS CORRECT.

Core Pilot possesses one further feature, which is that a jump forward in a program can be achieved by using an asterisk as a program marker. Then an instruction such as J:2 causes a branch to the second program marker forward from the jump. This is illustrated by the next program which converts figures to words.

```
    T:   ENTER THE FIGURE 1, 2 OR 3.
    A:
    M:   1
   YJ:   1
    M:   2
   YJ:   2
    M:   3
   YJ:   3
    T:   YOUR INPUT WAS NOT AS REQUESTED.
    S:
   *T:   ONE
    S:
   *T:   TWO
    S:
   *T:   THREE
    S:
```

Some reflection on these simple programs should quickly reveal that Core Pilot has some severe shortcomings: these led to the development of Common Pilot. With a good deal of ingenuity, programs to generate quite sophisticated dialogues can be written in Core Pilot, but a good author language for CAL ought to make it fairly easy to generate interesting dialogues.

Common Pilot

While Core Pilot permits the production of dialogues, it imposes an undesirable rigidity on the user's responses. For example, the first program in the previous section only recognises the correct answer when it is given in figures as '12', but 'TWELVE', 'Twelve' and 'twelve' are all equally correct, and they would be rejected. In the second example, the program will loop forever, continually demanding another attempt at the answer, if the correct response is not given. It is desirable to be able to maintain a counter so that after a certain number of attempts the correct answer can be given and the program can proceed. Additionally, it is useful to be able to deal with spelling mistakes in answers, for unless spelling itself is being tested, the continual rejection of correct answers that are wrongly spelt will be discouraging and perhaps even counter-productive in that it may lead the user to believe that a correct answer is incorrect. Some of these problems can be overcome in Core Pilot, but the extra features possessed by Common Pilot are designed to make it easy to tackle them, and other shortcomings.

The answer processing features of Common Pilot permit an answer to be matched against a list of possible forms of the correct answer, for example

M: 12! TWELVE! Twelve! twelve

where '!' represents the operator 'or'. A pseudo 'and' operator is also provided: it permits a long answer to be recognised from a list of its key words given *in the correct order*. To illustrate, the quote 'full fathom five thy father lies' would be matched by

M: fathom & five & father

as would 'at fathom five your father lies' and 'to fathom five thy father sank', but 'thy father lies full fathom five' would not match. An asterisk can be used within an answer to match to any single character in its position and so allow for simple spelling mistakes. The match instruction

M: sep*rate

will give a match to both 'separate' and 'seperate', as well as to 'sepprate'.

Other facilities of Common Pilot include computational instructions which start with a 'C' followed by a colon, and can then take the same form as a BASIC assignment, for example

C: COUNTER=COUNTER+1

It is made easier to write conditional instructions because a condition can be attached directly to any instruction, so that it is only executed when the condition is true, in the following way:

T(COUNTER<3): STILL WRONG. TRY AGAIN.

The jump instruction is also easier to handle, having the form

J: END

where END is a typical label, which is added to the instruction that is the target of the jump, in the form *END.

These are only some of the features of Common Pilot, but they reveal the way in which the designers of the language have tried to make it easier to write programs in Pilot. A direct consequence of the improvements is that Pilot programs have become more interesting to use, and much more flexible in the way that users can interact with them.

A program fragment intended to illustrate a typical test drill written in Common Pilot follows:

```
                   C:   SCORE=0
                   C:   COUNTER=0
*FIRST             T:   WHICH SAINT HAS A COCKLESHELL
                        EMBLEM?
                   A:
                   M:   JAMES! JAMES THE GREATER! SAINT
                        JAMES! ST JAMES
                   C:   COUNTER=COUNTER+1
                  YT:   YES. THE COCKLESHELL IS THE
                        EMBLEM OF ST JAMES.
                  YC:   SCORE=SCORE+1
                  YJ:   SECOND
J(COUNTER<3) :          FIRST
                   T:   THE COCKLESHELL IS THE EMBLEM
                        OF
                   T:   SAINT JAMES, THE APOSTLE.
*SECOND            C:   COUNTER=0
                   T:   WHERE IS THE SHRINE OF SAINT
                        JAMES?
                   A:
                   M:   SANTIAGO DE COMPOSTELA!
                        SANTIAGO! COMPOSTELA
                   C:   COUNTER=COUNTER+1
                  YT:   YES. THE SHRINE IS AT SANTIAGO DE
                        COMPOSTELA.
                  YC:   SCORE=SCORE+1
                  YJ:   THIRD
J(COUNTER<3) :          SECOND
                   T:   THE SHRINE OF ST JAMES IS IN SPAIN
                        AT
                   T:   SANTIAGO DE COMPOSTELLA
*THIRD             C:   COUNTER=0
```

With microcomputers so readily available in homes, schools and elsewhere, it is interesting to try to assess whether Pilot is a language capable of releasing their educational potential. Clearly, Pilot programs permit information to be presented and the user's assimilation of it to be tested. Since Pilot is a fairly simple language, it is not too difficult to obtain a working knowledge of it: having done this, teachers, for example, can then generate their own CAL programs to assist their current teaching. Various dialects of Pilot exist which incorporate features making it possible to draw on other resources that a micro may possess. MTC Pilot, as an example, gives access to graphics and sound generation, and permits subroutines written in machine code to be called. Such facilities widen the educational capability of the language besides ensuring that the user need never be bored.

It is significant that Pilot originated in a medical centre. Other interactive programming systems have originated from the medical environment, most notably programs for questioning patients, and accepting and analysing their answers in the same way as a doctor might. Programs of this kind can even diagnose the patients' illnesses, up to a point. Rather surprisingly, it has also emerged that some patients, after becoming accustomed to replying to a computer, prefer dealing with the computer to talking to a doctor! These programs incorporate discoveries and developments from the field of Artificial Intelligence.

This brings us back to Pilot, which does not permit too much intelligence (of any kind) to be displayed in analysing the answers that it accepts. Pilot seems to me to provide an *ad hoc* collection of techniques that can be applied in computer-assisted learning rather than embodying any consistent principles. The principles have been, and are being, developed, within Artificial Intelligence. Therefore, while computer-assisted learning programs can be written in Pilot, I feel that there is tremendous scope for improvement on them, and that superior systems for generating learning programs will inevitably emerge.

As a final comment, the naivety of Pilot as a computer language also shows in the total lack of structure that is characteristic of all Pilot programs as a consequence of having to construct all branches and loops using the jump instruction. For the same reason Pilot programs are no easier to read than assembly code programs.

Summary

Three languages, each of which is designed for a specific application that is widely used in the microcomputer field, are described in this chapter. The applications are computer graphics, robotics and computer-assisted learning. The uses of computer graphics range from the presentation of information in a readily assimilable form to the modelling of physical shapes in a simulation or a computer-aided design project. Robotics can be taken as representative of all the activities in which a computer is used to control another system rather than simply to compute. The computer's capability as a learning aid is potentially one of its most important activities.

There is considerable contrast in the structures of the three languages. As a graphics language GINO-F is a collection of subroutines, each of which can perform a specific graphics function. The notable achievements of GINO-F are to provide graphical output that is independent of any display device, and to provide two- and three-dimensional drawing commands in such a way that the two-dimensional commands are a logical subset of the three-dimensional ones.

The robotics language WSFN, although it contains commands specifically for robot movements, is a true computer language in the sense that it possesses all the facilities necessary for general-purpose computation. It is interesting as a minimal language in that it reveals how few features a language needs to describe any computation.

The features of Pilot are designed specifically for generating dialogues with a computer. Whatever one may think of the language, in turning the computer into an educational tool it opens one of the most important avenues in which computers can be applied.

Self-test questions

1.(a) Write a GINO-F program fragment to draw the four-sided shape shown in *Fig. 4.12a*.

(b) By invoking an appropriate transformation prior to replotting the shape, produce the compound shape shown in *Fig. 4.12b*.

(c) By invoking further transformations prior to replotting the original quadrilateral, plot the overlapping dodecahedrons of *Fig. 4.12c*.

2. How can the rotate and shift transformations be combined to produce a reflection such as the one illustrated by *Fig. 4.13*? (There are several ways of doing this.)

113

(A)

(B)

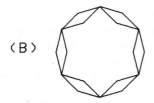

(C)

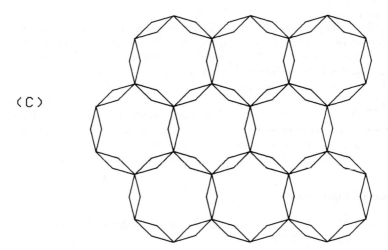

Fig. 4.12. Building patterns

3. Give the three-dimensional drawing commands necessary to describe the three-dimensional objects shown in *Fig. 4.14a* and *b*.

4.(a) Write a program in WSFN to cause a robot to follow a triangular path.
    (b) Write a WSFN program to cause a robot to follow the network

114

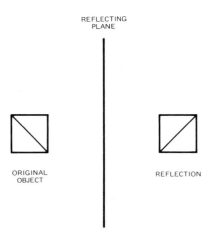

Fig. 4.13. Reflection

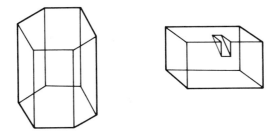

Fig. 4.14. Three-dimensional objects

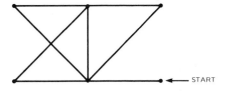

← START

Fig. 4.15. Network of lines to be traversed by a robot

of lines in *Fig. 4.15* without covering any line twice. Each line is 5 units long (units are stretched in diagonal directions compared to their natural length in horizontal and vertical directions).

5. A path can be traced through a maze such as Hampton Court maze, which has no completely disconnected parts, by keeping one's

right hand on the wall (or hedge) and proceding until the centre of the maze is reached. Write a program in WSFN under the control of which a robot can find its way through such a maze.

6. Write programs which use repetition that are equivalent to the following recursive WSFN macros. To have any observable effects, the macros must be run after the accumulator has been set to some non-zero value.
   (a) P=T(F−P)♭
   (b) Q=T(FR−Q)♭
   (c) M=T(AF2R−M)♭

7. Write a short Pilot program to test a student's knowledge of the important dates in English history. Give a tolerance of one year in accepting the dates. Simulate a typical dialogue that might result from running your program.

Appendix 1
Some other languages

There are other languages of relevance to microcomputers besides the ones treated in the body of this book. Brief discussions of some of them are included in this appendix.

Algol 60 evolved in the years around 1960, and the document entitled 'Revised Report on the Algorithmic language Algol 60' represented the culmination of its design. Algol 60 can be classified as a language for scientific computation. It can be used for other kinds of computation, but its lack of data structures, and in particular its rather limited facilities for handling strings and characters, makes it less than ideal for non-numeric computation.

Algol 60 was contemporary with FORTRAN and, as the first high-level languages, they were in direct competition. In contrast to the relatively *ad hoc* development of FORTRAN, Algol 60 was logically designed and formally defined in its report. Nevertheless, the outcome in terms of practical usage was overwhelmingly in favour of FORTRAN, particularly in America, although even there Algol was always favoured in academic circles. Academics favoured it, particularly in the teaching of introductory courses, because it lent itself to the practice of secure programming methods more than FORTRAN did. One of the objectives of Algol 60 was to provide a language in which computational procedures, or algorithms, could be expressed with precision. Ironically, despite the almost overwhelming use of FORTRAN, when the American Association for Computing Machinery (ACM) began to publish a section on algorithms in its *Communications*, it adopted Algol as the language in which they should be published. Algol 60 is still quite widely used, and implementations are readily available, with one in the CP/M library, for example.

Algol 68 is a separate language to Algol 60, conceived as a programming language in its own right and defined in its own formal report. It is a general-purpose language that is much admired in academic circles for its elegant design. However, it has proved difficult to implement fully, and its implementations are hardly sufficiently compact to be useful on current microcomputers.

The Algols have had a considerable influence on many subsequent languages, particularly as a result of their overall clarity and unity as languages, their block structure and control features, and the way in which they are defined. With the Algols, systematic methods of program development could be encouraged and well-structured programs could be produced. When Algol 68 was designed, it was developed from a small set of separate and independent concepts: it was also designed to be extensible, so that new operators and data structures could be defined as required and then used as part of the language. The subsequent languages whose designs were considerably influenced by the Algols include Pascal and 'C'.

The language 'C' is beginning to acquire a following among micro users. It has been described as 'an implementable Algol 68 and a Pascal that is not afraid to get its hands dirty'. The view of the language encapsulated in this description is one of a high-level language that can also give access to the hardware being used because it possesses a number of instructions that are equivalent to assembly code instructions. In this way 'C' can not only bring all the advantages of a high-level language but can also permit the hardware to be used to advantage. Typical applications of the language include systems programming and the type of engineering and control problems where a particular microprocessor needs to be used efficiently.

PL/1 is a general-purpose language combining the features and capabilities of both FORTRAN and COBOL, while showing the influence of Algol.

Logo is mentioned in Chapter 4. It has been put forward as an ideal first language to learn. There is an implementation of it for the Texas Instruments TI-99/4A microcomputer and, interestingly, the version of Pilot for the Atari microcomputers includes Logo-style Turtle graphics commands of the form

DRAW 10

and

TURN 90

118

Appendix 2
Further reading

Some suggestions for further reading on the languages covered in this book are presented here. For a particular microcomputer there will be certain information that can only be obtained from the manufacturer's manual, but the following references are recommended for all non-specific aspects of programming languages for microcomputers.

BASIC
Illustrating BASIC, by D. Alcock (Cambridge University Press, 1977).
BASIC for micros, by J. Maynard (Newnes Technical Books, 1983).

Pascal
Pascal user manual and report, by K. Jensen and N. Wirth (Springer-Verlag, 1975).
A practical introduction to Pascal, by I. Wilson and M. Addyman (Macmillan, 1978).
Pascal for micros, by Mike James (Newnes Technical Books, 1983).

COMAL and Pilot
There is very little to recommend on either of these languages. However, the magazine *Educational Computing* has included a number of short articles on both languages in 1981 and 1982.
Structured programming with COMAL, by R. Atherton (Ellis Horwood, 1982).

FORTRAN
A guide to FORTRAN IV programming, by D. D. McCracken (Wiley, 1972).
Programming in FORTRAN 77, by J. Ashcroft, R. H. Eldridge, R. W. Paulsen and G. A. Wilson (Granada, 1981).

Lisp
The little Lisper, by D. P. Freedman (SRA, 1974).
Lisp, by P. H. Winston and B. Horn (Addison-Wesley, 1981).

APL

APL/360: an interactive approach, by L. Gilman and A. J. Rose (Wiley, 1970).

PROLOG

'Solving problems in PROLOG', by R. Welham, *Computer Age,* August 1980, p59.

'Logic as a computer language for children', by R. Ennals, *Education Computing,* October 1981, p67.

Programming in PROLOG, by W. F. Clocksin and C. S. Mellish (Springer Verlag, 1981).

COBOL

COBOL programming, by J. Watters (Heinemann, 1970).

FORTH

'The evolution of FORTH: an unusual language', by C. H. Moore, *Byte,* August 1980, p76.

Threaded languages, by R. G. Loeligan (Byte Books, 1981).

Invitation to FORTH, by H. Katzan (Petrocelli, 1981).

Appendix 3
Answers to self-test questions

The answers to most of the self-test questions are given in this appendix. It should be stressed that when the answer is a program, the program presented may be one of many possible solutions.

Chapter 2

1.(a) X=A*B*C
  (b) W=A ↑ 2+B ↑ 2
  (c) Q=(X−Y)/16

2.(a) X:=A*B*C
  (b) W:=A*A+B*B
  (c) Q:=(X−Y)/16.0

3. The results printed out are 3 and 4.

4. 10   A=0
   20   B=1
   30   PRINT "NUMBER PROCESSING"
   40   INPUT X
   50   A=B+X
   60   B=A−X
   70   PRINT A, B
   80   IF X<>0 THEN GOTO 40
   90   END

5. PROGRAM PROCESSING;
     VAR A, B, X: INTEGER;
   BEGIN
     A:=0; B:=1; WRITELN('NUMBER PROCESSING');
     REPEAT
       READ(X); A:=B+X; B:=A−X; WRITELN(A, B)
     UNTIL X=0
   END.

6.(a) 10   INPUT X
     20   M=INT(X)
     30   S=(X−M)*60
     40   PRINT "THE NUMBER OF MINUTES IS", M

```
50   PRINT "THE NUMBER OF SECONDS IS", S
60   END
```

7.(a) The program computes and prints a number of values along the waveform $y = e^x \sin(2x)$.

(b) The program computes and prints the factorial of the entered integer.

(c) The program prints the string built up in A\$. This consists of the last pair of items in the string initially assigned to X\$, followed by the next-to-last pair and so on up to the first pair.

8.(a) TYPE LINE=RECORD
                         END1, END2: POINT
                  END;
        TYPE RECTANGLE=RECORD
                                   LINE1, LINE2, LINE3, LINE4:
                                   LINE
                         END;

Chapter 3

2. The function can determine if the item A is in the list L.

3. X←"INTELLIGENCE"
     4 ↑ 2 ↓ X

4. selection(paper).
     selection(stone).
     selection(scissors).
     win(paper, stone).
     win(stone, scissors).
     win(scissors, paper).
     tie(X, Y)←game(X, Y), X=Y.
     game(X, Y)←selection(X), selection(Y).

5.(a) DF   PFILE
              DATA RECORD IS POINT.
         01   POINT.
              02   XCOORD PICTURE 999.
              02   YCOORD PICTURE 999.
              02   ZCOORD PICTURE 999.

6.(a) 80
  (b) : CUBIC DUP DUP 3 + * 2 + * 5 + . ;

Chapter 4

1. The program that produced *Fig. 4.12(c)* is:
     PI=3.14159
     A=PI/6.0

```
      C=COS(A)
      S=SIN(A)
      X1=2.0*C
      Y1=2.0*S
      X2=X1+0.25
      Y2=0.0
      X3=X1
      Y3=-Y1
      X4=X1-0.25
      Y4=0.0
      CALL HP7220
      CALL UNITS(10.0)
      CALL SHIFT2(6.0*X1,6.0*X1)
      DO 10 K=1,3
      DO 20 J=1,3
      DO 30 I=0,5
      R=60.0
      CALL ROTAT2(R)
      CALL MOVTO2(X1, Y1)
      CALL LINTO2(X2, Y2)
      CALL LINTO2(X3, Y3)
      CALL LINTO2(X4, Y4)
      CALL LINTO2(X1, Y1)
30    CONTINUE
      CALL SHIFT2(2.0*X1, 0.0)
20    CONTINUE
      IF(K.EQ.1) CALL SHIFT2(-7.0*X1, 2.0+Y1)
      IF(K.NE.1)CALL SHIFT2(-5.0*X1, 2.0+Y1)
10    CONTINUE
      CALL DEVEND
      STOP
      END
```

2. If the distance between the object and its reflection is represented by X, shift the object by X and then rotate it about its centre by 90 degrees in a clockwise direction.

4.(a) HN6F3R6F3R6F

5. S(S(S(4RF)6RF)F)2RF

6.(a) AF
  (b) A(FR)
  (c) A(AF2R−)

7. The match statements in the Pilot program should be, typically, M:1065!1066!1067

Index